Martin Van Buren Moore

The rhyme of the southern rivers

With notes historical, traditional, geographical, etymological

Martin Van Buren Moore

The rhyme of the southern rivers
With notes historical, traditional, geographical, etymological

ISBN/EAN: 9783337238698

Printed in Europe, USA, Canada, Australia, Japan

Cover: Foto ©Andreas Hilbeck / pixelio.de

More available books at **www.hansebooks.com**

THE RHYME OF THE SOUTHERN RIVERS.

WITH NOTES HISTORICAL, TRADITIONAL, GEOGRAPHICAL, ETYMOLOGICAL, ETC. FOR THE USE OF TEACHERS, SCHOOLS, AND GENERAL READERS.

BY MARTIN V. MOORE,

Author of "Recollections of a Grey Jacket;" "Glimpses of Many Lands;" "Plantation Philosophy, or Idle Hours in a Darkey Cabin;" "The Christianity of the First Napoleon;" etc.

PUBLISHING HOUSE M. E. CHURCH, SOUTH,
BARBEE & SMITH, AGENTS,   NASHVILLE, TENN.

Entered according to Act of Congress, in the year 1897,
By MARTIN V. MOORE,
In the Office of the Librarian of Congress, at Washington.

THIS BOOK IS AFFECTIONATELY DEDICATED

by the author

TO THE GENIUS AND LOVE OF

HIS DEVOTED WIFE,

who, as

"BETSY HAMILTON,"

*has entered the Temple of Fame through the
Hearts of Millions
made happy by her Inimitable Literary Art.*

INTRODUCTORY.

THE RHYME OF THE SOUTHERN RIVERS, without Note or Introductory, was originally published in *Harper's Magazine* in February, 1883. As printed there, the Verses were imperfect and defective in some features considered essential. The aim of the author was to present in the Rhyme the correct name of every stream locally known as a "river" in the Southern states named. It was the purpose to give also, by means of the measure in the verse, the correct pronunciations of the respective appellations. The general directions and the chief characteristics of some of the waters were also introduced in the Verse.

Since the date of the original publication, in extensive personal travels all over the South, I have learned the further fact that there were also omissions of important character in the matter appearing in the magazine. The present writing embraces—with possibly a few minor exceptions—the names of every watercourse in the respective Southern states locally called "river." It includes also about fifty names which do not appear on the ordinary maps of the country. The pronunciations indicated in the revised forms agree substantially with the local expressions of the words.

The facts given in the Notes have been obtained after many years of careful research and inquiry. During the period covered by the labor on the work, I have not only visited in person every section of the American Union, going from ocean to ocean, and from gulf to lakes, gathering material bearing upon the native and prehistoric nomenclature of the continent, gaining in the mean time all the information now possible from the aborigines, the "red men" of the West, and elsewhere; but I have consulted every recognized authority to be found in the public libraries of Washington and other great cities.

The Notes are intended to throw some light upon the primitive tongue of the continent, and especially as it relates to the prehistoric names of the rivers of America. Thorough investigation of the subject has revealed the fact that the great majority of the original names of our waters now regarded as "Indian" appellations were not the coinage of the rude savages found here in the discoveries of the fifteenth and sixteenth centuries. The words appear to be survivals from a remote period. They appear also to belong distinctly to the tongue of the primitive peoples who first colonized the continent in the prehistoric civilization known to have once existed here, just as the river names of the Old World are the coinage mainly of the earliest colonists in the respective regions. The river nomenclature of the aborigines of America holds but little in common with the crude dialects of the modern natives. While the tongue of the historic Indian shows many hundreds of dialects without a well-defined maternity or unity, the river nomenclature of the primitive colonists—from one end of the continent to the other—quite distinctly reveals a common ancestry. And what is still more noteworthy is the further fact that this ancestry appears to have been coeval with various tongues of antiquity in the Old World. Innumerable striking likenesses exist in the prehistoric river names of America and those of prehistoric Europe and Asia. There is, indeed, a very long list of words that are recognized as native "Indian," of American birth, but which have accurate prototypes, and in identical connections, in the ancient languages of the Old World. Scores of the prehistoric river names of both Europe and Asia are reproduced in the prehistoric "Indian" appellations of America with such exactness and startling similitude every way as to forbid the acceptance of any theory which places the results in the domain of accidency. Some of the facts will be briefly referred to in the Notes of this work. The subject, however, is too profound and vast for full treatment in so unpretentious a volume as this is designed to be. "The gentle reader" who prefers to read only the Rhyme can quite easily skip the references to these Notes, while those who have no use for the mere verses may find much to interest and instruct in the prose of the appendages.

While I have endeavored to make the Verse attractive and entertaining, the obvious difficulties surrounding the subject should afford some shield in the matter of criticism. The work should not be judged by the usual canons of the art poetic. As the Notes are designed to represent historic truth in one special light, these—far above the Verse—have consumed my purpose and time most liberally in the writing. But it is through both Verse and Notes that I hope interesting and valuable results are to come to the reader.

The work is not offered to the public in any spirit of sectionalism; it is not the outgrowth of any mere sectional zeal or pride. Primarily, the idea of the book was of accidental parentage. In geographical studies, and in crossing numerous waters of the continent, years ago, I was impressed not only by the musical syllabication of the old " Indian " names; but there were constantly recurring terms or features in the native words which, in their common purposes, naturally suggested the common origin. This led to an investigation of the history of the words—an investigation which, as I have just observed, I have pursued with every possible advantage that could be obtained. While the work is purely original in its conception, as well as unique in its relation to American lore, I have not been alone in my theories in connection with the subject. One hundred years ago, nearly, that profound scholar and student Thomas Jefferson, in his book " Notes on Virginia," said: "A study of the native appellations of the aborigines of America will afford the best methods of arriving at the origin of that portion of the human race."

Mr. Jefferson's conclusions give the true key-note in the solution of one of the difficult problems connected with prehistoric America. The efforts of this volume can give but a glimpse of the subject. When we look for the " native appellations of the aborigines," we find them mainly, if not solely, in the ancient names of the waters of the continent. This statement is made in the conviction that analogous laws apply to the history of the human tongue in every part of the world alike. Most assuredly the very oldest evidences of the art and science of word-coinage come to us in river names. The first illustrations of this truth are seen in the names of the garden of Eden. These words still survive, while all other testimonials of the Adamic tongue have disappeared forever save as they were absorbed in the Biblical nomenclature and in the "confused" language of the post-Babel dispersion. The history of River Names shows that titles once properly applied to a water rarely ever perish. The river, or the water, has in all ages of the world been the boundary-line between nation and nation, and between man and man. The title at once became among the nations of antiquity a common heritage, a feature of the landmark as it were, which was to be inviolate—never to be removed. Hence the survival of the old names, until modern times, when in the vandalisms of civilized nations, many of the old words have been supplanted in order to give place to the "honorary" title. Many of the ancient appellations of America have been thus supplanted; but among those that remain there are hundreds which evidently represent the tongue of the first colonists who coined and applied the words to the various waters of the continent.

A very large and valuable collection of the old and native names of America comes originally from the Southern states. This fact is due to several causes. In the first place, the rivers here are very numerous—more so than in any other portion of the continent. I think I may safely say that three of the Southern states herein referred to contain more streams having the prehistoric name still known than any other similar area in the known world. Then, again, there are evidences of more thorough or perfect preservation of the aboriginal title than is seen elsewhere. This section of country appears to have been more thoroughly explored by thoughtful, unimaginative persons, whose journals of travel show clearly the native words, than were other portions. Nor were the ancient titles here subjected to that system of mutilation and suppression which has robbed our language of so many heritages of the aboriginal tongue of the new world. A few of the old native words come to us in the habiliments of poetic fancies. Many doubtless are lost forever. But the great majority of the primitive names of the waters of the South still survive in garbs which indicate substantially their once pure and native expressions. Many of the words now have forms that are known to be simply conjectural, and forms given without regard to any laws of uniformity in writing syllabic sounds.

In view of all these facts, this work is committed to the public not only as a study in geography and hydrography, but also as a contribution to philological science as this relates to the history of the aboriginal civilized man of America. MARTIN V. MOORE.

Auburn, Ala.

TABLE OF CONTENTS.

PAGE

Title-Page *1*
Dedication *3*
Introductory *5*
Where and How — Proem *13*
The Rivers of Virginia *15*
    Notes on, Page 17.
The Rivers of West Virginia. *23*
    Notes on, Page 24.
The Rivers of North Carolina. *26*
    Notes on, Page 29.
The Rivers of South Carolina. *39*
    Notes on, Page 41.
The Rivers of Georgia. *47*
    Notes on, page 49.
The Rivers of Florida. *53*
    Notes on, Page 57.
The Rivers of Alabama *61*
    Notes on, Page 63.
The Rivers of Mississippi *67*
    Notes on, Page 69.
The Rivers of Louisiana. *72*
    Notes on, Page 74.
The Rivers of Texas. *78*
    Notes on, Page 81.
The Rivers of Tennessee. *84*
    Notes on, Page 87.
The River Name: Its Origin and History *96*

WHERE AND HOW.

Where are all the rhythmic rivers of our sunny Southern clime,
Rivers named in Indian legend or in tongue of later time;—
Rivers quaint, or rivers mighty, rivers grand, or rivers wee;—
From the trickling o'er the pebbles, to the sound or gulf or sea?
  How do all their waters flow,
From their fountains gushing, through the mountains rushing
   Past the mosses and the ferns;
   Then, with tireless toil and turns,
  Dashing deftly, splashing swiftly;
Over cascades curling, in the pastures purling;—
Round through rugged rocky caverns whirling;
Over ledges lightly leaping, through the valleys softly sweeping
   Gracefully and slow;—
By the busy cities creeping, in the murky marshes sleeping
   Peacefully, dreamily and low;—
How through forest and the bayou wending,
With the Ocean and its myriads blending;—
   From the mosses and the ferns,
   How with ceaseless, tireless toil and turns
  Then do all these rivers flow
   To their sea-home
   With the sea-foam?
Where are heard their noisy numbers?
Where are kept their restless slumbers?—

—Listen how these rivers go.

NOTE.—The names of rivers are printed in CAPITALS. The figures given elsewhere refer to corresponding numbers in the Notes accompanying. Correct pronunciations are indicated by the measure of the verse.

THE RIVERS OF VIRGINIA.

Old Virginia north and eastward has POTOMAC blue and wide;
Northward lovely SHENANDOAH through the Valley pours her tide.
Southward sweep the dark BLACK WATER, deep MEHERRIN, NOTTOWAY.
Eastward ripples RAPPAHANNOCK, spreading into placid bay,
With a BACH and YORK historic, and the slow PIANKATANK.
Here are HAZEL, and PAMUNKEY with its dank and slippery bank,
Quaint OCCOQUAN and OPEQUAN, and MACHODAC, YEOCOMICO,
ROBERTSON and NASSOWADDOCK, ROCK FISH and the BUFFALO.
Here NEW, HOLSTON, CLINCH, and POWELL wind in meadows of the west;
Mingling in their merry music comes the welcomed mountain GUEST.
Here ELIZABETH comes kissing NANSAMOND and sisters ANNA,
RAPIDAN and MATTIPONY, and the rollicking RIVANNA.

PEDLER's here with SLATE and HARDWARE; and,
   still playing thus on names,
Let's go down the JACKSON, finding green COW PAS-
   TURE in the JAMES;
CHICKAHOMINY there meeting APPOMATTOX with
   their fames,
Finding NORTH and SOUTH united; here with sighing
   TYE they blend.
PINEY, WILLIS from its willows, and CALF PASTURE
   all here wend.
Here in ROANOKE gather STANTON, DAN, and moun-
   tainbright BLACK WATER,
BANISTER and SMITH and MAYO and HYCOOTEE,
   PIG and OTTER.—
Noble rivers! noble country! noble peoples! No-
   bler ones
Ne'er hath known the darkening shadows nor the light
   of circling suns!

NOTES ON THE RIVERS OF VIRGINIA.

	See Note		See Note
Potomac	1	Anna	7
Shenandoah	2	Rapidan	3, 12
Rappahannock	3	Mattipony	8
Bach	4	James	9
Piankatank	5	Tye	10
Occoquan	6	Roanoke	11
Robertson	3	Dan	12
Holston	151	Hycootee	13
Clinch	167		

1. POTOMAC. This word is variously written in old chronicles. It is found as Patowmek, Patomeka, Potomaque, and otherwise similarly. Many of the native Indian names now written with the final in "ac," "oc," "ock," and "uck" had originally an ending in a vowel sound similar to that heard in the pronunciation of "ee" or "A." As the final vowel sound was supposed by our forefathers to be merely the superfluous guttural of the savage tongue, it was in most instances suppressed or eliminated in the English writings of the words. The word Potomac shows striking analogy to the Greek term for river written *potamos*. This shows origin in the Sanskrit word for water, "Pa," and the Hebrew term for deep, "Te-ma," abbreviated from *Te-homa*. There are a number of the Indian names having prototypes in the Greek. See notes 45 and 103.

2. SHENANDOAH. This is really the Shannon-Doah, or Shannon-Toah, the final term "Toah" a well-known Indian word for river. The word has three forms in different dialects: It is found as "Taquah," as "Toah," and more briefly as "Tau."* The writing as "Ta-ho" is precisely the same original word. It shows origin in the germ-words "Te" and "owa," or "au," water, its literal significance that of deep water.† All the different forms are found in the names of deep waters in various parts of the world. As Ta-ho, it is the native name of a deep lake in California. In Spain there is a deep river having the prehistoric

---

*See Note 20 for "Tau." †See paragraph 4, page 99, for "Te."

title Ta-ho, the word appearing in the modern Spanish idiom as Tagus. In China the writing in English letters is Tai. The oldest form of the word is in the Hebrew in the writing Toah, in the name of a water, Neph-Toah. A term for water simply is found in many languages in the English writings "Owa," "Oah," "Owee," "Au-wa," and "A-haw." The old Teutonic form of the word is "A-wa," or in the Roman idiom "A-qua." This, in a composite with the root-word for the deep "Te," gives the form of the term as "Taqua" seen in the native names of many of the deep waters of America. Other forms of this word will be referred to in Note 61. The term "Shannon" in the Virginia name appears to be of more modern origin. It corresponds to the old Irish word Shannon, the name of a river in Ireland. Another old German word is reproduced in the name BACH. Note 4.

3. RAPPAHANNOCK. The term "Hannock" is found in another native name of Virginia, Tappa-hannock. Tappahannock is supposed to have been the old Indian appellation of the river now known as the Robertson. "Hannock," as a native term for river, was found in the dialects of both Virginia and California. The term "Rappa," seen also in the name Rappadan, or Rapi-dan, is supposed to be identical with the word seen as *ripa* in the Latin, the equivalent of *riva*. The term "Tappa" in the name Tappahannock, is referred to more fully in Note 116.

4. BACH. This is given as a native Indian appellation. It is curious that both Bach and Beck, seen in the aboriginal names of America, are also ancient Teutonic words for stream, the synonyms of brouk, or English brook. The Indian words are frequently seen in the writings Bog, Bogue, Boga, or Pogue, and Boca, these given by our authorities as native terms for stream or pond of water. See Notes 40 and 102.

5. PIANKATANK. Old writings give this name as Pyanketanke, with the final vowel sounded. The suffix "Tanka" or "Tanga" is a term found in the prehistoric names of waters in many parts of the world. An ancient Oriental form of the word as "Tong-ee" (written from the Turkish in English letters as Tengheez) is a term for lake. Mr. Stanley says that Tangani-ka in the Central African dialects denotes great lake. We find the term in the North Carolina name Pasquo-tank, and in

the Louisiana name Tang-apahaw. A brief form of the term is in our English word Tank, which denotes a deep enclosure of water. The remote origin of the term lies in a composite of the germ-word "Te," the deep, and the Oriental term for fountain, "Ain," in the strong nasal (French and Oriental) sound as "Ang" or "Ong," a sound heard also in the guttural form of the word as Kanga and Ganga and Congo. See Note 47.

6. OCCOQUAN. The aboriginal river nomenclature of America contains a term that has been variously rendered in our modern writings in such conjectural expressions as "Occo," "Aqua," "Auga," "Oga," "Ogee," "Uga," "Ouga," "Uckee," and otherwise similarly. The term is not confined to any particular section of the continent, nor to particular dialects of the natives. It has been found in widely separated regions, and in old dialects that had no known connections. In the Sioux, the term is given by authorities in the writing as "Au-gee," a word for river. As "Uckee," it is a Chickasaw term for water. In the sibilant form, as "Su-cah" and "Shoo-kah," it is found as a term for water and river in the dialects of both Virginia and California. See also Note 43. In the ancient Oneida tongue of New York, the word for water was written in English Oghua-canno. This expression may be regarded as precisely the same word which is seen in the writing of the Virginia name Occoquan, with its final vowel sound suppressed. Another native name in which the initial term "Occo" appears, and where its origin can be more clearly traced, is in the Georgia and Carolina appellation Occonee, in Note 25. The term appears as a parallel with similar words denoting water or river, and given in the English transcripts as "Ogha," from the Sanskrit; as "Accho," from the Hebrew; "Hugra," from the Greek; and as "Aqua," in the Latin, and "Acha," in the Celtic. These words, all appearing to have a common origin, are found in different forms reproduced in the native Indian names of America.

7. ANNA. This name does not owe its origin to that of the English Queen Anna, as has been supposed by many persons. It is a native Indian expression. It appears to be identical with the Hebrew and Persian term "Au-na," to which I have referred in the " River Name," paragraph 13. It is in various corruptions in all parts of the American continent. It is found most fre-

quently on the Atlantic coast, in such names as Riv-anna, Fluv-anna, Susqueh-anna, Lacka-wauna. The form as "Wau-nee," seen in the Pennsylvania name given, and the Florida appellation Suwannee, is in the South American name Cari-wauna. South America has the name also in the corruption Una, there being four rivers there with this name; one also named Una-Ri. In Turkey the writing is both Una and in the aspirate as Hanna. The aspirate form occurs also in the Spanish names Hain and Haina. The Russian symbols expressing the word in that language are rendered Yanna, Ianna, or Jana, and also Ona or Una, rivers of Russia. Mr. Stanley gives the form of the word Yeon as the name of a Central African river. The oldest form of the term comes to us in the Hebrew of two of the names of the rivers of Eden, Pash-au-na (Pison of the Anglicism in the Scriptures), and Gah-auna, or Gihon. The latter is seen in the French idiom as Guiana. Our Indian name Cheyenne appears to be identically the same word, this also in the French idiom.

8. MATTIPONY. This word gives the combined appellations of four small streams known respectively as the Mat, the Tye, the Po, and the Ny.

9. JAMES. This title was in honor of the English King James. Capt. John Smith, the early English explorer of Virginia, gives the native name of the river as Powhat-anna, the final term "Anna" referred to above in Note 7. The following are other native Indian names of Virginia rivers referred to in the journals of Capt. Smith and others; the identity of the respective streams now not positively known: Occam, Occobannock (hannock?), Namapona, Fluvanna.

10. SIGHING TYE. A remarkable physical fact is here connected with a historical occurrence. The North and South Rivers unite near Appomattox. In the combined currents the waters of the sighing Tye mingle. A "tie," one freighted with an immeasurable sadness, binds the two sections of our common country, North and South, and taking in an event at Appomattox, in 1865. Chickahominy and Appomattox are united in fame since then. Capt. John Smith writes the latter name Apamatuck. The term "Appa" or "Ap-aa" is known to have been used as a word for water or river in the native dialects of the continent. It remains yet in the tongue of the aborigines of

the Salt Lake basin as a term for water. Many of the old dialects had it in the corruptions "Ippe," "Epe," "Sepe," "Sippe," as well as in the modern writings in "Upa," "Oupa," and "Oppa." In the latter form it is seen in the Virginia name Oppe-quan, and the Louisiana name Opalousa (Opelousas of the French writing). Another reference to this ancient Sanskrit term Ap-aa, water, is seen in the "River Name," paragraph 12, and also Note 78. The term "Chicka," seen in the name of the Chickahominy, is referred to more fully in Note 164. The final in this name, "Hominy," is a native Indian word. It is found also as the appellation of a stream in North Carolina a tributary of the French Broad, the writing "Hominy." The word appears to be simply an aspirate form of the Hebrew name of one of the Syrian rivers, Aa-ma-na, or Ha-ma-na, the Abana of the Arabic. As Amana, the word is seen also in the name of a river in South America.

11. ROANOKE. This is not the true form of the native name. This modern expression has been evolved from the apparently doubtful writings of different early explorers who gave the word as Rowinoka, Roranoke, Owanoga, Orinoka, Oranoque, and otherwise similarly, in efforts to record the savage tongue. The word as Oronoko still survives in the name of the famous tobaccoes grown along the stream. The true prehistoric title was doubtless Orien-Ogha, or Orien-Aqua. The word appears to have been identical in origin with one seen as the native name of a river in South America, the word now written Orinoco. Identical physical facts are seen in connection with the two rivers: they both flow eastwardly for hundred of miles. The term "Orien" is an ancient word found in the languages of the Old World, and referring to the East, or to the direction of the sunrise. When the current of the Roanoke River changed its course, as it does in entering North Carolina, the natives no longer called it by the name "Orin-oka," or "Oronoko," but it was known as MORA-TOCKA or the MORA-TAQUA, the deep waters of the stream indicated by the term "Taqua," this referred to more fully in Note 61.

12. DAN is a true Indian name. The word is seen in another Virginia appellation, the writing Rapi-Dan. Other forms of the original word are seen in such native names as Catoc-tan, Yuca-tan. The history of the word has been referred to in

paragraph 14, the "River Name." DAN is one of the oldest river names known, it being conspicuous in Biblical annals, and also in the river nomenclature of ancient Europe, where it is seen as "Dan," "Don," "Doon," "Dun," and otherwise. The word is in the composite Dan-ube, this appellation appearing in the different European idioms as Don-au, Duna, Tanai, etc., the final syllables showing the identity of the terms for water in "Uba," "Au," and "Ai." The Latin form of the European name as *Dan-uwa*, or *Danuvius*, shows the German term for water written *awa* or *aha*.

13. HICOOTEE. The term "Cootee" is seen in a number of the river names of America. It is doubtless but a guttural form of the word for water or river as "Uda," referred to in Note 45. The term "Hi" is a superfluous aspirate expression, seen as the initial in such Indian names as Hiawassie, Hiawathie. It is seen also as a superfluous feature in the Edenic river name Hi-Dekel.

THE RIVERS OF WEST VIRGINIA.

Daughter of the Old Dominion! From her hills and mountain chains,
Swiftly gulfward pour her waters, through her pastures, vales, and plains.
Northward rush MONONGAHELA, green BUCHANAN, and the CHEAT;
In OHIO two KANAWHAS, GUYANDOTTE, and SANDY meet
PINEY, ELK, EAST, BLUESTONE, TUG, and GREENBRIER, HUGHES, BIRCH, and HOLLY,
CACAPAN, YEO-OGHA-NA, COAL, POCATALIGO, and GAULEY.—
Westward roaring, northward pouring, sparkling all in meadows gay;
Wandering, like an exile ever, here they scamper, plash, and play;
Ne'er returning for her greeting—from the mother run away.

NOTES ON THE RIVERS OF WEST VIRGINIA.

	See Note		See Note
Monongahela	14	Pocataligo	17
Kanawha	15	Gauley	18
Guyandotte	36	"Run away"	19
Yeo-ogha-na	16	Ohio	A

14. MONONGAHELA. Tradition says this native name means "river with falling-in banks." Central Africa has a river named Monongha. There are many identities in the native names of America and Africa. South Carolina has a Wando; Africa has a Lo-Wando—the prefix "Lo" a term for river in the African dialects. Other likenesses will be referred to in future notes. The term "hala" in the West Virginia name is duplicated in the suffix of the North Carolina name, Nantahala.

15. KANAWHA, written also KENAWHA. The word is said to denote the "river of the great woods or great canes." The term "Ken," or "Kan," or "Can," and Canna" is found in the prehistoric names of waters in all parts of the world. The oldest form of the word is in the Hebrew, where, as "Canae" or "Kenna" of the English writing, it is given as the ancient name of a river whose modern appellation signifies "the reedy," and hence our word "cane." The term is found in the native names of many American waters whose banks or shores have been noted for their extensive cane-brakes. In nearly every instance each one of the old appellations contains a well-known term for water or river. We have seen in Note 2 that "Aw-ha" is an ancient term for water.

16. YEO-OGHA-NA. This word is usually written in the grotesque orthography, Yough-oigh-e-ney. The suffix in the same is simply Occo-na. See Note 25. The term "Yeo" or "Ya" is the ancient word referred to in the "River Name, paragraph 2.

17. POCATALIGO. See Note 53.

18. GAULEY. This native American name is found also in many parts of the world. It is the same expression seen as the final in such names as Eaugallie, Ocala, Oghallah, etc. The

names Gaul, Galilee, and Wales all have the same remote origin, doubtless, as this American word. The most remote form of the original expression is seen in the Hebrew of the Edenic river name, De-Kau li, the Biblical Hiddekel, the Oriental Tegari or Tigris.

19. The rivers of West Virginia all run in an opposite direction from those of the mother commonwealth.

36. See forward, Note 36, for the term "Wye" or "Guy," as it appears here in Guyandotte.

A. The word Ohio appears to be simply a contraction or a corruption of a native name found in the journals of Columbus as Bohia—the name now written Bahia. The term "Hia" is seen in Hiawassie.

THE RIVERS OF NORTH CAROLINA.

Carolina! land of waters! Here the strangest rivers are:
ARRARAT and ALLIGATOR, and the famous stream of TAR!
Even FOLLY here is fleeing as a river to the sea;
Here are rivers FLAT and LITTLE as the waters well can be.
BROAD and ROCKY here are rivers; here are rivers old but NEW,
Yellow BLACK and silver GREEN, WHITE OAK, BAY, and REDDIE'S too.
Westward whirling wild WATAUGA, leaping ELK, and crooked TOE,
FRENCH BROAD (this the TAQUA-OSTA), and the wingless PIGEON'S flow;
TENNESSEE and swift HIAWASSIE, gulfward through the mountains go.--
From Virginia come MEHERRIN and the noiseless NOTTOWAY;
Out from Georgia little NOTLEY dances northward brisk and gay.
Where the Cherokees still linger is the nimble NANTAHALA.

In the land of Junaluskee is the VALLEE gurgling gaily.
In the dismal swamp-land is the viny-festooned SCUPPERNONG;
In the cloud-home and the sky-land SWANNANOAH skips along.
In the Smokies CATALOUCHIE lisps and warbles out in trills;
And the constant song of SENEKA the highland hollow fills.
In the pine-lands over marl-beds, ruby, wine-like CASHIE creeps;
In the fern-lands, 'neath the balsams, TUCKESEEGEE grandly leaps.
Here OCCONEE-LUFTEE laughs, and wee CHEEOWA frets and clashes;
'Mid her towering barriers LINVILLE (ESSEEOLA) spurts and splashes;
And the JOHN in foaming eddies 'neath the rhododendrons dashes.
In the gray and yellow hill-lands, where tobaccoes golden grow,
Tumbling DAN, and MAYO, FISHER, MITCHELL, and the ENO go.
Here is YADKIN (once SAPONA), winding mid a thousand hills;
Here's CATAWBA, pearly pebbled, from a thousand mountain rills.
Here's UWHARRIE with its hurry; here the lazy WACCAMAW;

Here are MILLS, and humming spindles on the busy DEEP and HAW.
Here in field and forest are the LUMBER and PEE-DEE;
And, borne upon her breast, COHERA, COLLY, and the MINGO wee,
CAPE FEAR'S storied waters—and these only—go to open sea.
Here CONTENTNEA and TRENT, pouring into NEUSE, find Okracoke;
Where the herring comes in spring time, are CHOWAN and broad ROANOKE;
NORTH and NEWPORT, YEOPIM, PUNGO, PASQUOTANK, and PIMLICO,
And PERQUIMANS, PANTIEGO, and SHALLOTTE— How they come and go!
Dripping, gurgling, rushing, tumbling, creeping—so they be—
Carolina's matchless rivers, from their fountains to the sea.

NOTES ON THE RIVERS OF NORTH CAROLINA.

	See Note		See Note
Tar	20	Yadkin	28
Folly	21	Catawba	29
Watauga	23	Uwharrie	30
Elk	40	Waccamaw	31
Toe	22	Haw	32
Taqua-osta	23	Pee-Dee	33
Pigeon	157	Colly	34
Tennessee	152	Cape Fear	35
Hiawassie	153	Neuse	36
Junaluskee	24	Okracoke	37
Swanannoah	38	Chowan	38
Seneka	49	Roanoke	4
Cashie	127	Yeopim	39
Occonee-Luftee	25	Pungo	40
Checowa	26	Pasquotank	41
Essecola	27	Pimlico	42
Dan	12	Pantiego	49

A number of the river names of North Carolina are referred to in the Notes pertaining to other states; hence the irregularity in the citations.

20. TAR. The origin of this name has given rise to much controversy. A few writers have supposed that it was but a contraction of the native word written *Torqueo*, or *Torpeo*, found in the region through which this river flows. It is known, however, that the true original name was not "TAR," but TAU. There was in the dialects of the old aborigines a term for water or river, and used in the appellative sense, but variously written in the conjectural orthographies of our early English and French colonists. Authorities give the form "Tau" as the word in the Uchee dialect, while for the old Apache dialect the writing is "Toah." A fuller form of the word is found in the writings "Taqua" and "Toccoa," or "Toquoy," as it is sometimes written. This is regarded as the Cherokee expression of the word, although it is found in localities outside of the range of that nation or tribe. The oldest known form of the word is, as we have already seen in Note 2, in the Hebrew, where it occurs in the name of a water noted in Jewish history, Neph-Toah. The word as "Tau" is the old Anglo-Saxon name

of a river in England. The term is found in all its forms in the prehistoric names of waters in America—both as initial and as a final—as in Choc-taw, Eu-taw, Pisca-tauqua, etc. See Note 61. As initial it is in the Georgia name Tau-aliga. Note 63.

21. FOLLY, usually known as " Lockwood's Folly." " FAU-LI," or "' FAU-LA," is a native Indian name, seen in the appellation Eu-fau-la. The name as Fau-li is also in South Carolina, a river appellation there. See Note 54.

22. TOE. This is an abbreviation of the true name ESTA-TOAH, the final term "Toah" referred to above in Notes 20 and 2. The term "Esta" is referred to in Note 154. A very remarkable fact in connection with the name Esta-toah is that it, or a word closely resembling it, is found in a book of travels in America, written and published in Venice before the discovery by Columbus. The work purports to be an account of the adventures of two Venetian sailors known as the Zeni Brothers. It not only describes the high mountain plateau of Western North Carolina near the source of the river named, but the name of the country is given as "Estote." Remains of stone houses described in the book are said to have been discovered also in Arizona. Corruptions of the name Zeno survive in the name Arizona, and in the title of an Indian tribe known as the "Zunis" found in that territory. While the word "Zuni" appears to be an exotic in American nomenclature, the term " Zona," or " Sona," is found elsewhere on the continent in the aboriginal appellations, and notably in the word Ama-sona, the native name now written Amazon, of South America, with its Hebrew "Am-aa" seen in so many of the aboriginal names of this country.

23. TAQUA-OSTA. The true word was doubtless Taqua-Esta, the final term found in a number of old Indian names not only as "Esta," but also in the known corruptions as "Osta" and "Ousta," as in the name written both Esti-nauli and Ousta-naula. For further reference to the term "Esta," see Note 154; and for " Taqua," see 2 and 61. TAQUA-OSTA is given as the old Indian name of the French Broad, the word said to signify " the racing river," a highly characteristic designation. The river was called French Broad at a time when it ran westwardly into what was known as the "French Possessions" of the country, and to distinguish it from the neighboring " Broad,"

which ran southwardly into the British territory of South Carolina. The French Broad has a tributary with the Indian name Hominy, referred to in Note 10, in connection with the name Chicka-hominy. See Note 150.

24. A remnant of the old Cherokee Indians still remains in Western North Carolina. Junal-uskee was a noted chieftain of the tribe. The term "Uskee," seen also in the name Sandusky, appears to be simply a corruption of the ancestral word whence come "uckee," "ouchee," "ousa," and a long list of similar writings having the significance of water or river, and found in the native dialects of America, Europe, and China.

25. OCCONEE-LUFTEE. In the native dialects of America there was a term for river which appears in the modern conjectural writings as "Occona," "Aquana," "Equona," "Oghana," or similarly. The old Choctaw form of the word is given as "Okina" or "Oceana," the latter now the native name of a waterfall on the river called Occonee, in Georgia. In South America the writing appears as Ocono. The name is found also in the Old World nomenclature. The very oldest form in which the likeness to the word appears is in the Hebrew of the Edenic name which bears the Anglicized version "Gihon," the name of one of the rivers of Eden. The true full writing of the Hebrew symbols in their English equivalents, with vowels supplied, gives the Edenic word Aga-auna, or in pronunciation Ock-a-au-na. This Hebrew name is evidently the remote ancestor of the Greek word Okeanos, the Latin equivalent *Oceanus*, our English word Ocean, and very nearly the pure Indian name *Oceana*. It is well known that the majority of our so-called Indian names are frequently in the mere conjectural writings. Unfortunately they have passed into official geography and history without any uniformity of phonetic expression. The words at times have been given the most grotesque guises, as though the tongue of "the savage" must needs be given a "savage" aspect. We see, for instance, the simple name "Ya-og-ha-na," showing the native term now under consideration, written on our maps and in histories as the Indian name of streams in West Virginia and Pennsylvania, and expressed in the letters Youghoigheney! "Luftee," in the North Carolina name, is a mere dialectic suffix, its significance unknown to the writer. The term "Occo-na," or "Aqua-na," is etymo-

logically the exact equivalent of Arabic Aba-na and Hebrew Ama-na, a Biblical name written in symbols which have the significance of waters which flow perpetually. (Isaiah, chapter lviii., verse 11.)

26. CHEEOWEE. This is a name which has been variously written and variously pronounced. What appears to be the same native word is seen in the English writings Keowa, Keeowee, Kiowa, and Kiawah. The latter is pronounced in some parts of South Carolina as Kee-wee and Kee-a-wah. I have heard the native Indians of the Pacific Coast use the word as "Ku-owa," it signifying with them "Big Water." Ku-owa is the aboriginal name of the Pyramid Lake, in Nevada. Kiowa is a name found also in the Russian.

27. ESSEEOLA. This is given as the native name of the river now called LINVILLE. The term "Ola" is doubtless the same as "Auli" or "Ou-li," the latter the Chinese form of the term, a word in the Mantchu dialect for river, and seen in many of the native names of American rivers. "Essee" is the same as "Assa." See Note 152.

28. YADKIN. "Yadkin" is not an aboriginal name, as has been supposed. It is merely a corruption of the old English appellation Atkin or Adkin. The stream was once known as "Adkin's River," the title coming from the name of one of the earliest European settlers on the river. "Yadkin" is a fanciful coinage. The aboriginal name of the river is said to have been Sapona or Sap-auna. See Note 7 for "Au-na." The term "Sap" or "Sepe" is seen in the native name of many American waters. "Sepe" a term for water or river, the equivalent of "Ippe." See Note 10.

29. CATAWBA. This native name is written also by our authorities Kataba. The same word occurs also in the Persian geography. It contains the old Persian term for water written in English "Au-ba," or briefly "Aub." The term is found both in purity and corruption in the prehistoric names of many different countries. France has the river names written both Aube and Ubaye. In the English transcripts of the Russian, we find the name as Obi or Uba, both forms reproduced in the native names of the rivers of America. There is an Obi river in Tennessee, the old writing Obey.* In the native names

---

* The name is now written also *Obed*. See Note in Tennessee Rivers.

of waters in South America the writing is both Uba and Ubi. The California writing is Yuba, this the name of two rivers there. The California writing reproduces the orthography given the term in its oldest forms in the Hebrew, where it appears in the word for river written Yu-ba-li. It is also seen in the old Egyptian name of the Nile written Yu-ba-ri, this the exact equivalent of the Hebrew term. It is supposed to be also the remote original of the old Basque term for river written Ibari, or Iberia of the modern versions. The form of the old term as "Ab-aa," denoting water, is in the Arabic appellation Aba-na, heretofore referred to in Note 10. The word is found in all its Old World forms in the aboriginal names of waters in America. The Latin corruption "uba," seen in the name Dan-ube, is in numerous Indian names of rivers.—Cat-auba is the river of the catfish. This variety of the finny tribe abounds in the stream from its mouth to its sources. So numerous are the fish in sections of the river that there is a belt of country lying along its banks in North Carolina called the "Catfish Township." I once asked an old Catawba Indian the question, "To which did the name Catawba first apply, to the tribe or to the river?" His answer was swift and convincing: "*Which was here first?*" The old natives did not call themselves "Catawbas." The original title of the tribe, the one by which they designated their nation, was the Usherees, the Way Openers, or the Pioneers. It has been the custom of our government authorities to call the aborigines by the native name of their chief water. In this manner nearly every distinct Indian tribe of North America has been designated, and this in some instances independent of the native titles. The old Cherokee name of the Catawba River was Inc-taqua, the term for "river" in the final "Taqua," this form of the word seen frequently in the appellations now regarded as "Cherokee."

30. UWHARRIE. This is simply the Ou-Warrie, or the river Warrie. The suffix "Warrie" is a term for river in different languages. In the French and Spanish writings we see it as Guarre, Garry, and also as Gare, as in the old writing Le-gare for the river now known as Lo-aire (Loire), the term Li or Lo, the root-word referred to in paragraph 1, the "River Name," and found in different languages as a word for river. The modern

Turkish form of the word is written in English Ghore, pronounced either Jar or Jor. This is the name of the stream which, with the Dan, makes the river Jor-dan, this name simply a composite of the titles of the two confluents of the river. The Hebrew writing of the Turkish name was Yeor or Yari. In the Russian the word is written either Jar, Iar, or Yar; in English letters, a term for stream or chasm. The oldest form known for the word from which "Warrie" has been evolved is in the Hebrew term written in English either Yeor or Yaa-ri, showing the germ-words Yaa, water, and Ri, running. Parallel forms are seen in the old Egyptian and Coptic in the English writings Aur, Airu, Eiro, and otherwise similarly. An ancient European form of the word, and known as a "Celtic" term for river, is Aar, or Aa ri. All those river names of Western Europe which are now seen in the writings Ayr, Ayre, Aure, Ohre, and Or, are supposed to be due to the Celtic origin, in the term Aar, and this traceable to the Egyptian form of the word as Aur. An ancient Chaldee form of the word was Ur or Ure, this the Chaldee name of the Euphrates, the term used in the appellative sense. The word occurs also in the Hebrew as Ureah. The Chaldee form of the name is in the French appellation of a river, Eure. It is in a number of the aboriginal titles of waters in America. Alone, it is the name written Ouray, a river of Colorado, and as Ouri, the old name of the San Jacinto, of Texas. In composites, it is in the names Miss-ouri, Ura-guay, of South America, and in other native appellations. The old Celtic form of the term as "Aar" is seen in our names Aar-Kansas, Aar-oostook, Aar-apahoe, Arre-dondee, and others. The term as "Warrie" is in the native name of one of the Tennessee rivers having the modern title, Wari-ota, now the Cumberland. See Note 148. The synonymous features in the name Oo-warrie are referred to in paragraph 10, page 101. See also paragraph 8.

31. WACCAMAW. The term "Maw" in the Indian appears to have had the significance of "great water." See Note 93. The word as Mah, or Mo, was in the ancient Chinese a term for the sea; it is yet in the Hebrew, the generic word for water. The name Waccamaw refers primarily to the lake Waccamaw.

32. HAW. This is another abbreviation of the native names

of North Carolina. The original word was SAX-APA-HAW. This is supposed to have been the Indian name of the Cape Fear. It is a curious and interesting fact that the term "Sax" seen in this and other native names of America, and which is the Sanskrit root of the Latin term *saxeum*, rock, is found in the names of some of our rockiest rivers. There are three forms of the root-word, *sca*, *ska*, and *sax*. Our authorities give the former as a native Indian word denoting rocky, a synonym of the Latin *saxeum*. The Haw and upper Cape Fear are the rockiest rivers in North Carolina. The Potap-sca is the rockiest in Maryland. The Penob-sca (Penobscot in the French idiom) is the rockiest in Maine. The Sax-achawan is the rockiest in British America. Two of the rockiest streams in Florida have in their native names the term "sca," the Pithlacha-sca-te and the Chassahowit-sca. The Thronade-sca of Georgia is so proverbially rough and rocky that it has been called in modern parlance the "Flint." In addition to the Sanskrit term "sax," seen in the North Carolina Indian name Sax-apa-haw, it contains also the Sanskrit term for water, "Apa," found also in many other native names of America, not only in purity, but in the corruptions "Ippa," "Epe," "Sepe," etc. See Note 10. "Humming Spindles." Several of the largest cotton-mills of the state are on the Deep and Haw Rivers. MILLS is a river name in the state. The word "Haw" in Indian appears to be a term for river, the exact equivalent of Hebrew Hai, Chinese Ho, and the Teutonic A-haa, these words denoting river.

33. PEE-DEE. There has been some doubt as to whether or not this is a genuine native name. The most trustworthy evidences are in support of the declaration that it is a true aboriginal title. Its two distinct terms are found in numerous other native names. "Dee" is in the near-by name Sand-dee (Santee), the term "Sand" found also in Sand-usky (Note 24) and in Santaffee of Florida, besides in other native names. "Dee" is the root-word referred to in the "River Name," paragraph 4. In the old Anglo-Saxon tongue the term was used in the appellative sense as the name of deep waters, the Scottish corruption being "Tay" and "Tye."

34. COLLY. This name is supposed to be etymologically the same as the word Gauley, referred to in Note 18.

35. CAPE FEAR. In the old colonial records this name is

written "Cape Fair." The native appellation is given as Sax-apa-haw. (Note 32.) Of all the many rivers of North Carolina, this is said to be the only one going directly into the open sea, the others emptying into "sounds," or leaving the state through other territory.

36. NEUSE. "Neuse" is an abbreviation of the native name originally written Noos-Ooka. "Ooka" is a dialectic expression of the true word Ogha, or Aqua, referred to in Note 6. The name Neuces, of Texas, showing the French idiom, is doubtless the same as the North Carolina word.

37. OCRACOKE is the native name of a "sound" or inlet on the eastern coast of North Carolina, which receives the rivers named.

38. CHOWAN. The name was originally Cho-wanna, the final vowel eliminated in the modern writings. The word, and the names Shewannee, Suwanee, Swannanoah, and Savannah are supposed to be all corruptions of one remote, original, sibilant form of an ancestry whose Hebraic type is in the name Ama-na, waters flowing perpetually. It has been conjectured that the native sounds as "Su-aa," heard in the initial of the names, have for their origin the remote root whence comes our words "sweet," "suave," etc. Traditions connected with the names Suwannee and Swannanoah appear to confirm such a supposition. It is well known, however, that the old Oriental terms for water or river in the English writings (Tcha, Chu, Tsai, Su, etc.), are seen in the native names of the waters of the continent. The Turkish term Su is the name of one of our rivers, the French form of the writing being Sioux. See Note 165.

39. The term "Yeo," or "Yaa," seen in the prehistoric names of so many of the American waters, is an ancient germ-word or term for water, and found well-nigh universally in prehistoric river names. Further reference is made to the word in the "River Name," paragraph 2. Our authorities tell us that in the ancient language of Mexico the word for water was in our symbol A, as it was in the old Swiss, with the sound of O, the same as the French word written Eau. The old Saxon form as Wye is found not only as the name of waters, but it is in numerous composites, such as Wye-oming, Wye-ota, Y-reka. The form of the word as "Ya" or "Yeo" is not con-

fined to any special dialect or any particular section of America. A form of the word as "Yu" is also found, not only in the Hebrew, but in America also, as in Yukon, Yucatan, Yuma. The latter, which is a correct Hebraism of the word given in the Mosaic annals as the appellation of the Deity for the "gathered waters" of the creation, its equivalent "Yoma" most frequently used, was the ancient Indian name of the Colorado River, of California. The ancient germ-word as "Ya" is seen in the names Yakima, of California (and which is precisely the same etymologically as Waccamaw), in Ya-hooli, Yali-busha, and in many others.

40. PUNGO. This is another abbreviation of an original name. The full word, as given by early explorers of Eastern North Carolina, is written Matcha-pungo, or Metche-pungo. The initial is doubtless the same word we see in one of the old names of the Mississippi, Metche-Sepe, seen also in the name Michi-gan and its Mexican duplicate Michioagan. (See Note 130.) The term "Pungo" is an Oriental word found in the nomenclature of Asia. Another Oriental word found in North Carolina names of waters is the Chinese term for lake written in English Bogue. Bogue is a noted sound in the eastern part of the state. Our authorities say that Bog, Pog, and Pang are words for lake or pond in the native Indian dialects. There are various orthographies for the words. In Alabama is a creek with the native name Esta-boga, the term "Esta" referred to in Note 154. In South America is a deep water, its native name Bog-ota. The Indian words as Bog and Pog are strikingly like the old German terms for stream written Bach and Pach. There is a wide variety of expression given the Indian word Pog. It is seen as Poca, as in Pocataligo (Note 53), Poca-hontis, Loacha-poka, etc. As Poga or Pogue it was found as the name of a water in Western North Carolina, supposed to have applied originally to the river now called the Elk. The stream is now called Elk from the fact that the last survivor of this noble animal in the South Atlantic states was killed on the head waters of the river early in the present century by the late Col. William Davenport, of Caldwell County, this state.

41. PASQUO-TANK. The term "Tanga" has been referred to in Note 5. The term "Pasquo" is seen also in the name of a river in Mississippi. Note 118.

42. PIMLICO. The names Pimlico and Palmlico appear to signify waters of the palm or the pine.

43. There is in North Carolina a creek known as the "Sugar." The old native title was SUCAH. Capt. John Smith, in his journals of travels in Virginia, gives the expression "Sucah-auna" as a native term for water. The initial is doubtless the same word which Mr. Bancroft gives as Shoo-kah as one of the native terms of the Pacific Coast—a word for water. In Brazil, the same native expression occurs in the name of a river, the Suca-rio, or simply the Sucah River. In Georgia is a creek called the Sucah-noochee, sometimes written Suckernuchee.

THE RIVERS OF SOUTH CAROLINA.

By the rice-fields and the sand-hills run the rivers small and great,
From the mountains to the ocean in the grand " Palmetto State:"
From SAVANNAH on the westward, to the eastmost WACCAMAW;
By CATAWBA, where the red man once untroubled kept his squaw:
Bubbling, hurrying, foaming, splashing, gently, smoothly then they flow;
Once they find her sunny borders ne'er across them do they go.
PACOLET, SALUDA, REEDEE, TYGAR, BROAD, BUSH, ENNOREE,
CONGAREE and WATEREE, all in SANTEE, seek the sea.
To SAVANNAH, CHAUGA, LITTLE, SENEKA and TUGALO,
KEEOWEE and TAXOWAY, and the rattling ROCKY go.
To the ocean COOSAW-HATCHIE, lazy LYNCH, and dark CHEHAW,
ASHLEY, COOPER, these in Indian ETOWAN and WASMASAW.
Eastward flowing is the COOSAW; by the islands EDISTO;

By the cypress SALKEE-HATCHIE and the POCA-
   TALIGO.
By the countless fields of cotton, spread the small and
   great PEE-DEE;
Here, the sea waves kissing, SAMPIT, BROAD, MAY,
   WRIGHT'S and CHECKASEE.
Here are FAULEE, BULL and HARBOR, and the way-
   ward WADMELAW,
MORGAN and the small KIAWAH, and the darkened
   OWENDAW.
Here are BLACK, once WINNEE, sleepy STONO and a
   NEW,
COMBAHEE and sluggish WANDO, and the narrow
   ASHEPOO.—
From SAVANNAH west and southward, from the east-
   most WACCAMAW;
To CATAWBA, where the Indian still is living with his
   squaw;
From the rich hills to the barrens, busy rivers small
   and great,
Run by factory and plantation in the grand " Palmetto
   State."

NOTES ON THE RIVERS OF SOUTH CAROLINA.

	See Note		See Note
Waccamaw	31	Wasmasaw	51
Catawba	29	Salkee-Hatchie	52
Pacolet	44	Pocataligo	53
Saluda	45	Pee-Dee	33
Tygar	46	Faulee	54
Congaree	47	Kiawah	51
Wateree	48	Winnee	55
Santee	50	Combahee	56
Seneka	49	Wando	57
Keowee	26	Savannah	58
Coosaw-Hatchie	64	"Living with his squaw"	59
Etowan	51		

44. PACOLET. This appears to be a version, in the French idiom, of the true word Pacola or Pa-Kauli. For the term "Kauli" see Note 65.

45. SAL-UDA. This is the leaping water. The river in fact leaps over many high places in its course from the Blue Ridge to the sea, giving numerous fine water-powers. The term "Uda" in the name shows striking likeness to the Greek *Udor*, the Sanskrit *Uda*, and the old Slavonic *Woda*, words denoting water. The most remote form of the word is seen in the true Hebrew of one of the names of Eden, the English writing in Au-de-Kau-li, or "Hiddekel," as it appears in the Biblical writings. The term "Au-de" signifies briefly deep water. It is used as the name of a number of deep rivers in the Old World. In France the writing is *Aude*, while in the names of Italy it appears as *Adda* and *Adi*. The term is seen most frequently in the native names of America in the corruptions "Ota" and "Uda," "Ute," or "Oo-taw." The name Utah applies originally to a deep lake in the territory of this name. A name that appears to be kindred to Saluda is Salaqua (or Salaquoy, as usually written in the river names of Tennessee). The initial term "Sal" appears also to be kindred to the Latin *Salio*, to leap, and whence comes our word "sally."

46. TYGAR is given as a native Indian name. It shows like-

ness to the Oriental river name Tigris, or Te-ga-ri as it appears in its most remote form, the meaning simply deep water running, and just as the Semitic form of the name, De-kau-li, signifies deep water flowing.

47. CONGAREE. This musical Indian appellation has many interesting likenesses in the river nomenclature of the Old World. The expression is simply "Conga Ri," or Conga River, the aborigines of the continent who named its waters having had knowledge of the term "Ri" as a word for river. This statement is made on the authority of De Soto, who gives the term "Ri" as one of the native names of the Mississippi. Countless mere verbal facts are also in support of the statement. The word "Conga" or "Congo" is itself an Oriental term for river, it being one of a group of words in which are embraced the Sanskrit Ganga (Ganges) and the Chinese Kang-hi or Konki, all with similar significance, river or great water. A Spanish form of the word is Concho, this the name of a river in Texas.

48. WATEREE, an Indian name showing the term "Ri" in a composite with the Orientalism, Arabic Wady, or "Wattie," as our native names show it. It appears in the Alabama name Coosa-Wattie, and also in the South-American appellations showing the Spanish idiom in the writing Guatimauli, Guati-vita, etc.

49. SENEKA. This aboriginal word, found in New York and South Carolina, has its exact prototypes in the Old World nomenclature. The American name, however, doubtless antedates that of the noted Roman consul. And the river name Senegal is also doubtless prehistoric. The true form of our Indian word is evidently SA-NI-KA, the term "Ni-ka" a corruption of a remote original of which the Hebrew term for river, Na-ka-ri, or Nachar, is the highest and purest type known. This old Semitic term is reproduced in a variety of writings in the ancient names of the waters of the world. We see it in the German river appellation Neckar. It is in the African names Niger and Tanga-nika. We see it also as the initial in our Central-American name Nicar-augua. Our Indian term "Nooka" is evidently a low corruption of the word. There appears to have been in the primitive tongue of man a word for water having the sounds of the English letters "e-cuh,"

"ee-ka," or "ee-ga," the writing frequently in "i-co," or "i-cho," as seen in the name Jericho. This latter name, we know, owes its origin to the "exuberant waters" found about the site of the city. The ancient term appears to have been used by the Russian language-makers in the coinage of their term for river written in English either raga, rega or rika, simply running (Ri) water (Ga or Ka). The primitive term is reproduced in the old Latin *equor*, or *æquor*. We see it also in the Hebrew word for river written fully Aa-pa-li-ka (peleg), this a word reproduced exactly in the Indian name Opelika. Nowhere in the world is the ancient primitive term "ee-ka" found with more frequency and certainty than in the Indian names of the waters of America. We shall have occasion to refer to the facts again. The old term has been given such a wide variety of verbal expressions having identical sounds that we shall have no difficulty in recognizing it in the native Indian words.

50. SANTEE. This name is doubtless Sand-dee, Santee a proper euphemism. See Note 80 for "Sand," and for Dee, in the "River Name," paragraph 4, page 99.

51. ETOWAN and WASMASAW are given as the Indian names of the ASHLEY and COOPER Rivers. The latter was known also as the KIAWAH (*Kee-wah*, in pronunciation), the name now belonging to another and near-by river. See Note 26. Original titles have been changed in numerous instances, the words applying to different waters. We need not wonder at this, since most of the ancient appellations had no other significance than that of river, or water under its varying conditions. While different tribes had apparently different titles to the waters, it has been found that the words themselves are near identities. The South Carolina name is usually written ET-I-WAN, while the similar appellation of Georgia is written Et-o-wah. If we follow the old Anglo-Saxon orthography in writing the suffix, the true form of the name would be Et-a-wan. Our authorities give the term "Awan" as identical with "Avon," "Abon," "Abhan," and "Aban," old words for river in a number of the now obsolete dialects of Western Europe and the British Islands. The term as "Aban," or "Abon," appears to be simply an abbreviation of the Arabic word given as the Biblical name Aban-aa, the equivalent of Hebraic Amana, whose original characters are rendered elsewhere in a transla-

tion as "waters which flow perpetually." See Note 25. The words Habana and Havana are doubtless due to the same remote ancestry which gives us Abana, the former in the aspirate Spanish idiom. It is a further curious fact which shows that prototypes of the two native American names referred to, Etiwan and Etowah, are also found in the British Islands in the prehistoric names written Etawah and Etive.

52. The term "Hatchie" is an old Seminole word for river. This and the non-aspirated form of the word as "Atchie," or "Acha," are found in many parts of the continent in the native names of waters. They are found also in regions supposed to have been unknown to the old Seminole tribe, whose original domains were in the Florida peninsula and in the near-by bordering territory. Corruptions of the term exist in the writings "Uchee," "Ouchie," "Houchee," etc. The purest form of the word known is in the old European (Celtic) term for river written Acha, and as Aci in the Italian. See Note 169.

53. POCA-TALIGO is found as a river name in West Virginia also. It is a pure Indian word. The term "Poca" is doubtless the same word we have seen in Note 40. The term "Taligo" appears to be kindred with the word Aa-palika referred in Note 49. A corruption of the word is seen in the writing Tellico, Note 159. Jellico and Jericho are also apparently cognate names. The name Pocataligo applied not only to the river, but it was also known as the title (derived from the original river name) of a noted Indian village on the water, long famed as one of the "cities of refuge" among the aborigines. This ancient Mosaic institution, cities of refuge where accused criminals should have protection and an asylum, appears to have been well known among the old natives of America. One of the last of these Indian cities to disappear in the historic era was situated on the Tennessee River. See Note 151.

54. FAULEE, written also FOLLY. See Note 21.

55. WINNEE. "Winnee" is the wine-colored. This is the native name of a river now called the BLACK, from the color of its waters, which are of a rich wine hue. The term "Winnee," seen in a number of the old native appellations of waters in Northern states and in British America, signifies, in the supposition of many writers, the muddy or the turbid. The color of the "WINNIE" in South Carolina throws strong light

on the problems connected with the word. The waters of the Lake Winne-pisc-aqua, or Winne-piskoga, as sometimes written, are not colored; they are bright, and unusually clear and sparkling. The term "Winne" in this name does not, therefore, appear to refer to the waters of the lake, but to the intermediate factor in the name, the expression "pisc." The waters of the lake have long been celebrated for their fine wine-colored salmon and trout. The inference is therefore clear that the name Winne-pisc-aqua was originally intended to denote *the waters of the wine-colored fish*. This interpretation carries with it the supposition, if not the fact, that the aboriginal philosopher who coined the expression "Winne-pisc-aqua" had knowledge of the Latin words *pisca* and *wina* (vina). Many facts are in support of such a theory, but the limits and purview of these Notes forbid any extended discussion of the subject. There is, however, no doubt of the fact that there are scores of terms and full words in the aboriginal nomenclature of America having not only exact likenesses in the Latin and Greek, but the common significances of the expressions appear to be also identical. This fact goes far to remove the question or fact of likeness from the sphere of mere accidency. The river and water nomenclature of prehistoric America shows no term with more frequence than that which we see in the forms of the Latin term for water, *aqua*. The word *pisca*, which is not known to antedate the Latin, is seen again in its purity in connection with the Roman term *aqua*, in another native appellation, Pisca-taqua, this the name of a lake one of whose tributaries was so noted for its fine fish that even in historic times it has received the title " Salmon Falls River."—It is worthy of note in this connection to state that in the book of the " Zeno Voyages," referred to in Note 22, the Italian authors say that even at the time of their visit to this new world (or "island," as they called it) there were Latin books still in existence here. And Mr. Prescott, the historian of the Mexican conquest, says that, at the time of the occupation by the Spaniards, Roman games and Roman sports and the Roman system of notation were known and practised by the natives. The cross as a symbol in religion, not known anterior to the crucifixion of Christ, has been found in various parts of prehistoric America, the fact evinced in the famous " Lorrilard Collection " of relics in the Smithsonian

Institution, at Washington City. The ruins of a temple dedicated to the Triune God, not known in any age anterior to Christ, was also discovered near the city of Mexico. Other Latin terms seen in the names of Southern rivers are referred to in Notes 130, 154, 45, 67, 126, 158, 100.

56. COMBAHEE. A local pronunciation gives the name simply "CUMBA" or "KUMBEE." The final term "Hee" is doubtless but the mere word for "river," the equivalent of Chinese and Hebrew "Hia," and seen also in the Indian name Hia-wassie. The term "Cumba" is seen in the native Alabama names Tuscumbia and Escambia

57. WANDO. Wando is an Oriental word for the sea. It is also the exact equivalent of Sanskrit Hondo, Indu, Sindhu, Inde, and Aande. The name India (pronounced "Ond" in French idiom) has the same origin. The ancient term is found in the prehistoric nomenclature of America; all its Old World forms are reproduced in our native names. As Wando, it is not only in the South Carolina appellation, but it is found in the original title of a stream in Pennsylvania, the To-wando. As Lo-Wando, it is in Central Africa, the term "Lo" a word for river. The term as Onte, Onde, or Aande is in the native names of a number of our deep waters, illustrations seen in the writings Ontario, On-anda-ga, Onte-rocti or Aande-rocti, this latter the Indian name of Lake George, in New York. The aspirate form of the word is in the names Honduras and Hondo, of Texas. The ancient term as Aan-de or On-te, owes its origin to the germ-word De, the deep, in a composite with the Oriental expression Ain, En, or On (paragraph 13, the "River Name"), the word signifying simply deep, perpetual water. The oldest forms of the true word are seen in the Hebrew in the names of the ancient city Anti-och, on the banks of the river Aar-onte (Orontes).

58. See Note 38 for Savannah.

59. CATAWBA. See Note 29. A remnant of the old Usheree or Catawba Indians still live on a reservation in York and Lancaster Counties in this state.

THE RIVERS OF GEORGIA.

From the mountains on the northward, how do Georgia's rivers go?
How, to Mexique Gulf and Ocean, do her waters fall and flow?—
From the silvery CHATTAHOOCHIE to the golden ETOWAH,
To the broad and grand SAVANNAH, by the deep ALAPAHAW;
From the turbid OCCLOCONEE to the crystal TUGALO,
From CHATTOOGA to SAINT MARY'S, Georgia's rivers come and go.—
Northward TENNESSEE, HIAWASSIE, NOTLEY, and TOCCOA pour;
Here's ULAFFIE'S liquid laughter; here TUROREE'S toss and roar.
Here are HERB and FENHALOWA, WILMINGTON, and WILLACOUCHIE,
TYBEE, NEWPORT, and OCLOCKNEE, CROOKED, TURTLE, SUWANOOCHE,
OKEEWALKEE, and the SOQUE, and the tiny TESNATEE,
And SUWANEE, oozing from the fens of Okee-fenokee.--
Here the CHESTATEE goes chafing round and o'er the rocky steep;

Here OGEECHEE, TOWALIGA, and the two SAUTILLOS creep
Through the barrens by the cypress and morasses dank and deep. -
TALKING ROCK and COOSA-WATTIE, SALAQUOY, and ELLIJAY,
OOSTENAULI, CONNESAUGA,— six in COOSA roll away.
Here are BROAD, ALCAUFAU-HATCHIE, SAUTEE sauntering, AUCHEE-HATCHIE,
Leaping, terrible TALLULAH, olden NEW, and APALACHA.
Here is FLINT, once THRONADESCA; here CANOUCHIE'S cany tide;
Here OCMULGEE, dark and murky, ALTAMAHAW, deep and wide;
SAPELO and HANNA-HATCHIE, sluggish MEDWAY, bright YAHOOLA;
LITTLE, once OCCOLOC-OOCHIE, TALLAPOOSA, and PATOULA;
OCCOPILCO, and OCCONEE, and OCCOA, clear and small;
ICH-A-WAY–NOCH-A-WAY, and AMICOLOLA, with its brawl;
WITHLAC-OOCHIE, and WELAWNEE, and the CHICKASAW, and all—
From the CHATTAHOOCHIE chattering, to SAVANNAH murmuring low,
Where is heard the OOHOOPEE:—so Georgia's rivers sing and go.

NOTES ON THE RIVERS OF GEORGIA.

	See Note		See Note
Chattahoochie	75	Tallulah	67
Alpahaw	121	Thronadesca	68
Hiawassie	60	Canouchee	69
Toccoa	61	Hanna-Hatchie	70
Tybee	116	Yahoola	71
Okee-fen-okee	62	Occoloc-Oochie	72
Towaliga	63	Tallapoosa	73
Sautillos	101	Patoula	71
Coosa-Wattie	64	Occonee	74
Salaquoy	158	Occoa	76
Oostenauli	65	Savannah	77
Connesauga	103	Oohoopee	78
Alcaufau-Hatchie	66	Nochaway	B

60. HIAWASSIE. This is a short river, but its waters are in three different states. It is referred to more fully in Note 153.

61. TOCCOA. This word is variously written, as Tocoa, Tuccoa, Toquoy, Tockoi. It is the same native word which we find as a term in the writings Taqua, Tauga, Daigua, Tioga, and in the corruptions and abbreviations "Tock," "Toga," "Tuckee," etc. A type of the word, as Tokoi, is found not only in the Hebrew, but also in the Japanese. The significance of the word appears to be simply deep waters,—its origin in the term *aqua*, water, and the germ-word *tc*, the deep. The word "Occoa" is an Indian corruption, the equivalent of *aqua* or *ogha*. See Note 6. The Toccoa was known also as the Aquokee.

62. OKEE-FEN-OKEE. There are various pronunciations of the name of this great swamp of Southern Georgia. The native accent is usually on the last syllable of their words. It is a remarkable fact that in the old Indian names of swamps, and of some rivers in low, marshy regions, there is found the old Celtic word for swamp, "fen." The names Okeefenokee, Fenhalowa, and Econfenee are illustrations—the latter a Florida appellation. The term "Okee" is a well-known native word for water or river, it being a pronunciation of the Sanskrit as *ogha*, or a corruption of the Latin as *aqua*. See Note 6.

63. TOWALIGA. The suffix "al-iga" in this name is referred

to in Note 53. The initial *To* or *To-ah* is doubtless the term *Toah* referred to in Notes 20 and 2.

64. COOSA-WATTIE. The term "Wattie" in this name has been referred to in Note 48. It is evidently a real "term" in the full sense of that word, and the exact equivalent of the Arabic Wady and Spanish Guade. The term is dropped from the name of the tributary, and the river becomes simply the "Coosa" in the lower part of its course in this state. The word "Coosa" is found in different Southern states as the name of rivers. In South Carolina it is rendered "Coosaw." As "Coos," the word is also in the New Testament. In the native dialects of America the word appears to be simply a guttural form of the term *Usa* or *Ouse*, meaning river. See Note 24.

65. OOSTENAULI. See Note 154 for the term "Oosta." The word Nau-li is a Hebrew term for river, doubtless the remote original of the name Nile. In the ancient Hebraic MSS. the form of the word is expressed in the symbols corresponding to English N-L, the usual writing Nahal or Na-auli. We find the term as "Nolly" in the Indian nomenclature. See Note 154.

66. ALCAUFAU-HATCHIE. The modern abbreviation of this true name is written "Alcova," the term for river, "Hatchie," dropped.

67. TALLULAH. This word is said to mean "the terrible." The physical facts as well as the verbal truths are well in support of the tradition. The word appears to owe its origin to the Latin term *terrere* as *tellele*. The old Cherokees, from whom the word comes, did not use the letter R in their dialects, hence the form of the word as *tellele*, this also a legitimate form of the Latin, the old Romans using the letters R and L interchangeably. The briefer terms "Tella" and "Talla," seen so frequently in the (Cherokee) Indian names, must be regarded as having a different origin. The Indians appear to have used these terms *Talla*, *Tella*, and *Tulla* in the sense of "muddy" or "earthy," and hence these words appear due to the Latin as *terre* or *tella*, earth. See Note 73.

68. THRONADESCA. This was the native name of the river now called Flint. The late Dr. David Reese, of Georgia, whose father was one of the early pioneers of the country, gives the name also as FLEENADESCA or FLEENATESCA. The term "Throna" occurs in the native name of a lake in Florida.

The term "Sca," the final in the names, is referred to in Note 32.

69. CANOUCHEE. See Note 15 for the term "Can," and Note 72 for "Ouchie."

70. HANNA-HATCHIE. The term "Hanna" is simply an aspirated form of the word "An-na," as in the name Susquehanna. The two synonyms in the word are explained in paragraph 9, the "River Name." For "Hatchie" see Note 169.

71. YAH-OOLI. For the term "Ya," seen in this name, see Note 39. The word Ou-li or Ula, seen in so many of the native river names of America, is a parallel form of the term Ou-ri or Ura. The oldest forms of the word are in the Hebrew and the Chinese. In the former it is written Uleah, the name of a water. In the Manchu dialect of China the form of the word as Ula or Ouli is a term for river. The word as Ya-li in the Chinese is the same which we see in the English writings as the Yellow (Sea) and Yellow (River). The identity of the terms Ouli and Ouri is illustrated in our Indian names Missouri and Missouli, the same word in different dialects, many of the old Indians rejecting the sounds of the letter R. See Notes 67 and 147. The word as *Tu-lee* is found in the Indian nomenclature.

72. The Indian name of the Little was OCCOLOC-OOCHEE, the initial term seen also in the name OCKLOCK-NEE. Oochee, or Uchee was the old Muscogee word for river. There is a creek in Georgia and one in Alabama having the name simply Uchee. The tribe of Indians known as Uchees received their title from the Alabama name. Uchee is a corruption of Acha. The word is found in one of the old dialects of the British Islands, a term for river, the ancient writing *Uxe*. See Note 169.

73. TALLA-POOSA. The term "Talla" is supposed to signify the "muddy" or the "earthy." Note 67. It is found in the native names of rivers whose banks, caving in, give the muddy or earthy character to the waters. The suffix "Poosa" contains the old Anglo-Saxon term "Usa," the initial P supposed to indicate in the Indian tongue, as it did in the old Roman language, the idea of "powerful." See Note 103.

74. OCCONEE. See Note 25.

75. CHATTA-HOOCHIE. The term "Chatta" is given as an

old Choctaw and Cherokee name of the owl, the pronunciation expressing, in an onomatopoetic sense, the notes of the bird, and just as the word Wi-on-ias-sa in the Osage tongue meant whippoorwill.

76. OCCOA. The name is written on old maps as *Aquo-ke* also. See Note 155.

77. SAVANNAH. See Note 38.

78. OOHOOPEE. This is the river ("Ooh," or "Eau") UPA or OOPEE. The word Oupa is a well-known corruption of the Sanskrit term for water, Ap-aa, referred to in paragraph 12, the "River Name." The corruption is conspicuous only in the river names of Russia and America, although found elsewhere in the appellations of waters. Russia has a river whose name is written either Oupa, Upa, or Oopa. One of the rivers of California appears to have had the name originally as "Hoopa," in the Spanish writing, the title preserved in the name of an old tribe of Indians who lived on the waters of the stream. This is evidently the name we now have in the English idiom as *Yuba*. There are two rivers in California with this name. We see the term as "oupa" in the suffix of the Texas and Spanish appellation Guadeloupe. A parallel form, as well as a congener, of the word as Upa, is seen in the writings Uba and Yuba. See Note 29.

B. See Note C, page 60, the "Rivers of Florida."

THE RIVERS OF FLORIDA.

Where the orange grows and gladdens, and the summer softly sleeps,
Florida in summer stillness all her many rivers keeps:
From PERDIDO bordering westward, to SAINT MARY's eastern flow;
Through the hummocks and the pine-lands, turning, creeping, there they go:
Who that e'er has seen them wonders why the Spaniard loved them so?—
Where the swan and water-eagle make their brooding and their nest,
AMAXURA and the CHARLOTTE there go crooking to the West;
Westward wind the WEEKEEWATCHIE, WITHLACOOCHIE, SANTAFFEE,
Tampa's HILLSBOROUGH, MIAKA, and the PITHLACHASCATEE,
ITCHEE-PUCKEE-SASSEE, HAMMOTH, roving ROGERS and a NEW,
CHOCKOLISCEE, CORK-SCREW, twirling with an ALLIGATOR too!
Softly southward sweeps SUWANNEE, sweet SUWANNEE, famed in song,

In melodies that echo still the vanished olden tongue.
South flow Alaqua, Ocilla, Saint Marks, Apalachicola,
Choctaw-Hatchie, Shoal, Escambia, Occoloconee, and Chipola,
Attapulgo, Crooked, Brother, and Alapahaw, Waucassie,
And Sopchoppy, and a Little, and the wandering Waukeesassa.
Southward glides the small Talooga; so Waukulla winds away;
So Black Water, Econfenee, New and Yellow, and the Bay,
Fenhalowa, and Stein-Hatchie where the waves with mosses play.
Westward creep the Cootee-Hatchie, Anclote, Alafiah, Pease,
Chassa-howit-sca, Apopka, Crystal, Salt and Manatees.
Eastward crawls the gray Opossum, Saint Sebastian, Little, North,
Lemon, Bell and Jupiter, and Jolly, Snake, there stealing forth;
Nassau, Halifax, Matanzas, and Saint Lucy, Eaugallie,
Middle and Hulpatiokee and Amelia, Miami,
Econtock, Tomoka, Turkey, these all soughing to the sea.

Out from Okee-cho-bee's marshes, hot CALOOSA-HATCHIE steals;

Out from lake-lands fair, KISSIMMEE all her wondrous wealth reveals;

Out from bright, pellucid fountain, fountain deep and pure and wide,

HOMOSSASSIE'S crystal currents, matchless marvels, gulfward glide;

Out in coquetry with ocean, lags the tawny INDIAN'S tide;

Out from hummock rich and gloomy, home of bruin and of deer,

Gulfward winds the wee WAKIVA, dancing, sparkling, bright, and clear.

Northward RITA runs to lake, where the lazy current sleeps;

Out from OCKLAWAHAW northward, grand SAINT JOHN to ocean sweeps.

Out go ALCATOPA, HARNEY, GALLIVANT, from Everglades,

With WAHLIKA, FAHKAN-HATCHIE, neath the somber palm-made shades,

With CAXIMBAS, CHITTA-HATCHIE, these all wandering in the South,

Where the SHARK is throwing open from the gloom his murky mouth.—

O'er the sands or reefs, here broadening into ocean, gulf, or bay,

Where the countless wild fowl gather there to dream
  the years away;
Where the orange grows and gladdens, and the summer nods and sleeps,
Florida in summer stillness all her drowsy waters
  keeps;
From PERDIDO bordering westward, to SAINT MARY'S
  eastern flow;
Past SUWANNEE sung in ditties, murmuring ever
  soft and low;—
Who that e'er has sailed there wonders why the Spaniard loved them so?

NOTES ON THE RIVERS OF FLORIDA.

	See Note		See Note
Amaxura	79	Eaugallie	90
Santaffee	80	Miami	91
Hammoth	81	Econlock	92
Suwannee	82	Tomoka	93
Ocilla	83	Kissimmee	94
Escambia	107	Homossassie	95
Talooga	84	"In coquetry with ocean".	96
Econfence	85	Ocklawahaw	97
Stein-Hatchie	86	Itchee-puckee-sassee	C
Anclote	87	Waukulla	D
Apopka	88	Rita	E
Saint Lucy	89	"In Summer Stillness"	F

79. AMAXURA. This is an old native name of a river now commonly called the larger WITHLOCOOCHEE, there being two rivers in the state with this latter name. There are also two called New and two Manatee. The name written "Amaxura," with its term "Ura" referred to in Note 30, is doubtless the same aboriginal word written Amaccura, a river in South America. There are numerous identities in the native names of the two sections of the continent. H. H. Bancroft, the historian, who has given the subject long and careful investigation, says, in his work on the native races of the continent, that all its dialects reveal a common origin. The term "Ama" in the names cited is referred to in paragraph 4, the "River Name."

80. SANTAFFEE. This is the true native name. It is not Santa-Fe, of the Spanish ecclesiasticism. The terms "Sand," or "Sant," and "Affa" are in other Indian appellations. See Notes 50 and 24.

81. HAMMOTH. This name occurs also in the Hebrew.

82. SUWANNEE. This celebrated Indian appellation is referred to in Note 38.

83. OCILLA. This native Indian name is also written AQUILLA. The word evidently has the same origin of the Biblical appellation Aquila, the name of one of the companions

of St. Paul, the likenesses accidental doubtless. The name is found also in African nomenclature.

84. TALOOGA. This is doubtless a corruption of the original whence come the writings Taligo and Tellico. See Note 53. The modern Indian writing gives the word as Tallaquah, a city of the Indian Territory.

85. ECONFENEE. This writing contains the term "Econ," or "Ecan," which is doubtless the same as that seen as the final in such native names as Michigan, Wauregan, Oregon, etc. The term "Fen" is referred to in Note 62.

86. STEIN-HATCHIE. This old Indian name has as its initial the German word for stone, *stein*, in connection with the Seminole term for river, the writing "Hatchie," seen so frequently in the names of the rivers of this state, the old territory of the Seminoles. See Note 169.

87. ANCLOTE. This word is pronounced locally in two syllables, the accent on the last, and in long sound of O, as An-clōte.

88. APOPKEE, usually written CALOOS-APOPKA. The word "Caloosa," "Calusa," or "Colusa," seen in the native names of two of the Florida rivers, is also a native California appellation, the old title of the river now known as the Sacramento, this a name showing the influence of the ancient Spanish priesthood there. "Cal-usa" means hot water, or warm water, both physical and verbal facts in support of the declaration. The term "Cal" is referred to more fully in Note 147; "Usa," in 73, and elsewhere in these pages.

89. SAINT LUCY. The true word is doubtless not the ecclesiasticism "Saint Lucy," but SAND-LOUSA. The term "Lousa" is found in the native Indian name of waters not only in Florida, but elsewhere. Florida has the lake name Loch-loosa, the term "Lack" occurring also in the name Lackawanna. The term "Lousa" is referred to more fully in Note 170; the term "Sand" referred to in Note 80.

90. EAU-GALLIE. This name contains the term "Gau-li" referred to in Note 18. Different versions of the same original word are found in the Wisconsin name written Oghalla, and the Florida city name Ocala.

91. MIAMI, with accent as Mi-am-ee on last syllable. This native name is found also in Indiana and Ohio.

92. ECONTOCK. The true word is doubtless ECAN-TAQUA, the final vowel omitted in the modern expression. " Ecan " is referred to in Note 85; Taqua, in Note 61.

93. TOMOKA. This appears to be a corruption of the word as TE-MAQUA, or more fully TE-MA-AQUA. Ma-aqua is the aboriginal name of the river now known as the Hudson, of New York. The title still survives in the corruption " Mohawk," the name of one of the tributaries of the Hudson. George Bancroft, the historian, says the word Ma-aqua denoted simply " The Great River." It may be worthy to state that the germ-word as " Mah " is given as the old Sanskrit root of the Latin word *magnus*, great. The aborigines had a corruption of the expression, Ma-aqua, which we now see in the writing " Muckee," denoting, in the native mind, " Big Water," the term seen in the lake name Winne-Muckee, and in the old Cherokee title of the Tennessee River as Kalla-Mucky. See Note 164.

94. KISSIMMEE, pronounced locally as Kis-sim-ma, the accent on the second syllable. Kissammo is in European geography.

95. HOMO-SASSA. This and the Tarpon Springs are among the most remarkable of the many phenomenal waters of the state, this a wonderful realm of fountains, lakes, and unique streams. The term " Homa," found also as Aa-ma or Am-ah, Yo-ma and Homa in the Hebrew, where it was used to denote waters under various conditions, as seas, lakes, rivers, and harbors, has been referred to in paragraph 4, the " River Name."

96. " In coquetry with ocean." The Indian river approaches very near the Atlantic in several places before finally yielding its current to the embrace of the sea.

97. OCKLAWAHAW. This is the native name of a river now called the SAINT JOHNS, the true word now applying to the water which is the source of the main stream. OCKLAWAHAW is given as a Seminole word denoting, in the native tongue, simply " flowing waters." Its ancestry is seen in the germ-word Li, or La, and " Ock " and " Waha " waters. See paragraph 1, the " River Name," for " Li."

C. It will be observed, doubtless, by the reader, that there are in the names of a number of the rivers of this state terms or features not held in common with the majority of the expressions of the Indian nomenclature of other parts of the country. Such expressions as "Itchee," "Withla," "Pithla," "Hulpa," "Fahkan," and others peculiar to the water names of Florida, evidently belong to the modern dialects of the country, and not to the tongue of the primitive colonists. Most of the lake names of the state appear to be of the modern coinage also. The dialectic expression "Itchee" is seen also in the Georgia name *Icha-way-Nochaway*. The name *Ichawur* occurs in Oriental nomenclature.

D. In the old Spanish this is written *Guaxula*. The word is precisely the same thing etymologically as Eaugallie, referred to Note 90—"Kulla" a corruption of Gaulie and "Wa" the Teutonic equivalent of French "eau."

E. *Rita* is an ancient Old World word for river or deep running water. Corruptions exist in Reda, Rood, Ruth, Rotter, and otherwise. The Dutch name Rotterdam shows the term; this the "dam" on the Rotter, or the river.

F. "In summer stillness." There are but few of the rivers of Florida the murmur of whose currents can be heard at the distance of a dozen yards.

There are a number of the river names showing corruptions of terms and other expressions that have been so frequently referred to in the previous Notes that I have made no immediate references to them here. The likenesses to the ancestral types suggested will be readily recognized and located by the reader who has read the work continuously thus far.

THE RIVERS OF ALABAMA.

Where the Indian, fleeing southward, hard by Northern foemen pressed,
Found a hunting-home in peace, is ALABAMA: "Here we rest!"
Past PAINT ROCK and FLINT here came he; over sucking, tumbling TENNESSEE;
Over WARRIOR (TUSCA-LOOSA), down CAHAWBA did he flee;
Leaving ELK, LOUK-SAPA-TILLA; seeing SIPSEE; crossing COOSA:
Past TOMBECKBEE, OAKNOXUBEE; paddling pretty TALLA-POOSA;
Past SEPULGA, and CHATTOOGA chattering nightly as an owl:
BUTTA-HATCHIE, SUARPOKEE, PATSILIGA, and the FOWL:
Roaming by the NEW and LITTLE, over North and CHOCTAW-HATCHIE,
Past the RED and bounding DEER, and the prattling APALACHA:
Then in peace he rested; hunted; fished he then in HILLABEE;
In CONECUH, YELLOW-WATER, CHOCTAW-HATCHIE, STYX and PEA;—

Fished in waters fringed with mosses in the glades, KANTAPPAHAW,
And ESCAMBIA, BONSECOUR, and TENSAW, FISH and CHICKASAW.—
From the border by PERDIDO, to the eastmost ESCATAPPA,
Over MOBILE in its beauty, fishing, hunting, dreaming, happy—
Here the Red Man, fleeing southward, hard by lakeside foemen pressed,
Found the game and grave forever! ALABAMA! Here they rest!

NOTES ON THE RIVERS OF ALABAMA.

	See Note		See Note
Alabama,		Talla-Poosa	103
"Here we rest"	98	Chattooga	104
Flint	165	Butta-Hatchie	105
Tennessee	99	Hillabee	29
Tusca-Loosa	100	Conecuh	49
Cahawba	29	Kantappahaw	15, 116
Louk-Sapa-Tilla	101	Escambia	56, 107
Coosa	64	Bonsecour	106
Tombeckbee	102	Escatappa	107
Oaknoxubee	29	Mobile	108

98. ALABAMA—"Here we rest." There is a belief that the name ALABAMA meant, in the Indian tongue, "Here we rest." It is said to have been a joyful exclamation of an oppressed people who, fleeing southward from their more powerful foes of the northern lake regions, found a resting-place on the banks of the Alabama River. It has been recently claimed, however, in the interest of historic truth, that the so-called "legend" is but a bit of clever and innocent fiction, emanating solely in the brain of a distinguished son of Alabama, still living and honored as a poet and a jurist. The coinage, however, is so replete with graceful and poetic fancies, and withal so well in accord with historic possibilities, if not historic truth itself, that I shall not only give it a lodgment here, but I endeavor furthermore to picture the flight of the oppressed over the different waters of the northern part of the state, leaving them, the aborigines, fugitives no longer, in the blissful existence of hunting, fishing, and paddling along the other waters of the central and southern part of the state. I shall add this much more, for the benefit of readers who have a fondness for the curious in word-lore. The name Alabama, which is unquestionably a native appellation, contains apparently two distinct terms which are not seen in any other river name of America. These are "Alla" and "Bauma." The latter is a well-known ancient word regarded as the remote type, if not the ancestry, of the English word "balm." The original word denotes anything that soothes or delights. The writing "Allah" is the

name of the Mohammedan Deity, the equivalent of the Hebrew ELOI, the true God. The historian, Prescott, calls attention to the instances in which the Greek name of the Deity, THEOS, and the Latin DEUS, occur in the language of the ancient Mexicans. The knowledge of the ancient philosophers who named the waters of the continent appears to have embraced many curious and startling features that are not chargeable to accident except in the trespass upon reason. The name of the leading character worshiped by the Brahmans, Buddha, is also found in the Indian appellation of one of the rivers of Alabama, the word written as BUTTA-HATCHIE, the dental sounds on the native tongue never so perfect or distinct as to enable the hearer to determine clearly the enunciation, whether it expresses a T or a D. Illustration of this fact is given in Notes 50 and 147. The word "Butta" is not found elsewhere in the Indian names of America, at least so far as my researches have extended. The occurrences may be all accidental. I give them "for what they are worth"—no more.

99. "Sucking, tumbling TENNESSEE." The reference is to places in the Tennessee River that are known to boatman and others as "the sucks." These are dangerous localities along the "Mussel Shoals" where the current seethes and boils and tumbles over the immense ledges of limestone that obstruct the flow of the waters. Rafts and boats are frequently drawn under the current in these "sucks." There are other points on the river known as the "Frying Pan," "The Skillet," "The Pot," etc., referred to in other Notes (147, 152). The word "Tennessee" is not pure Indian: it is a fanciful writing of the original name Ten-assa. The Cherokee name of the river was Chal-aqua or Kal-aqua, sometimes written in old works Kellakee.

100. TUSCALOOSA. This is the native name of a river now known as the Big Warrior or Black Warrior. The great chieftain of the Tuscaloosa tribe of Indians was killed on the banks of this river in 1540 in battle with the Spaniards under De Soto. The slain leader was a warrior with a very black skin; and in consequence of the fact he was referred to by the white Europeans as the "black, black warrior," this name appearing on the oldest English maps of the country. The title of the tribal chieftain came from the native name of the river. See

Note 29. The term for river in the word is in the expression "Loosa," which owes its origin to the ancient term for water "Ousa" and the germ-word "Li," the flowing. See Note 89. There are many striking facts connected with the term "Tusca," seen in this Alabama name. It is found originally in the prehistoric names of our waters only in a narrow belt of latitude stretching from the shores of the Atlantic, where the old Tuscarora Indians had their hunting-grounds, to Arizona, where it ends, the last apparent survival in the name written in the Spanish idiom Tucson. There are so many evidences of the Roman knowledge possessed by the ancient aborigines of the continent that it has been conjectured that the word "Tusca" seen in the native American nomenclature is reproduced from the ancient Latin name Tusca, which once applied to the Roman province now known as Tuscany. The word appears to have been left in the New World by some early explorers and colonists, and as the memorial of their fatherland. From time immemorial it has been customary for new colonists in virgin countries to fix in the nomenclature of the country some memento or testimonial of the ancestral home or the ancestral tongue. The migrations of the ancient Celts and Moors, and various other peoples, have been followed and traced over the Old World simply by the shreds of their tongue left in the prehistoric nomenclature of different regions. In like manner the old French and Dutch and Spanish and German colonists of this continent have left mementoes of the mother tongue in every locality where their influence was long felt. The term "Tusca" has some curious connections. Tusca-ora means literally a native or inhabitant of Tusca. The Tuscarora Indians were said to be "shirt-wearers." Possibly the ancient garments brought from the fatherland gave rise to the tradition.

101. LOUK-SAPA-TILLA. The term "Tilla" is simply *De-la*, the deep flowing. It is in the Georgia name Sau-tilla. "Sapa" is sepe. (Note 10.) "Louk" is an unknown dialectic term.

102. TOMBIGBEE. The river is now usually referred to in the abbreviation "Bigby." The true native name was "TOM-BECK-BEE. (See Note 4 for "Beck.")

103. TALLA-POOSA. (See Note 73.) The term "Tallah" is supposed to mean "muddy" or "earthy." On the Tallapoosa River is a noted waterfall having the native name "Talassa."

This word is strikingly like the old Greek term for the sea, *Thalassa*, this showing origin in the germ words Te as "Tha" in the Greek idiom, and Li and assa as "lassa." The pure form of the term we have seen in the Indian corruption "Lousa." "Te" is the deep; "Li" is the flowing; and "assa," water—the deep-flowing water—a brief, yet comprehensive, designation of the sea. See paragraph 6, the "River Name," for fuller reference to the germ-words named. See also Note 170 for Lousa.

104. CHATTOOGA. For the term "Chatta" see Note 76.

105. BUTTA-HATCHIE. See Note 98 for "Butta," and 169 for "Hatchie."

106. BONSECOUR. This is evidently an original word in French idiom.

107. ESCA-TAPPA. This is the native name of the river called DOG or CEDAR on some of the maps. The term "Esca," seen also in the prehistoric names of America as "Esque" and "Eska," is found also in the Hebrew in the names Esca-lon and Aska-lon. It is also in the old Irish and Welsh in the writings Aesca, Isca, Uisque, and otherwise, with the significance of water or river. The original writing of the name Wisconsin shows one of the old Irish forms of the word, Ouisque-onsin. The word "whisky" owes origin to the Irish form of the word. The term "Tappa" is doubtless the same original word we have in the Indian nomenclature as "Tippa." The oldest form of the word known is in the Hebrew name of a water En-Tappuah, now called simply Tappuah. See Note 116.

108. MOBILE. The Indian name was originally written Maubela or Maubile, and also *Mauvila*.

THE RIVERS OF MISSISSIPPI.

All along the west meandering, here, far up, full MIS-SISSIPPI,
Restless monarch, always marvel, from his burdened mossy lip he
Out on live oak and magnolia bottoms prodigally spills
A SUNFLOWER, once SOCK-TAFFA-TOOTA; TALLA-HATCHIE from the hills
Eastward drinks it with COLDWATER, changing into YAZOO where
YALLA-BOOSHA and LOOSA-SCOONA seek the flitting "Father" there,—
They and BLACK and HOME-CHITTO, and, from bayou, deep PIERRE.
Northward in the knob-lands, TIPPA, WOLF, and HATCHIE hie away;
Loitering LEAF, FOX, BUCKATOONA, in the far south seek the bay.
PASCA-GOULI, CHICKASAWHA, with the TULLA-HO-MA blending,
And BOUGH-HOMA, slowly southward darkened currents here are sending.
O'er eastern borders ESCA-TAPPA and OCKTIBBEHAW here break;
Here NOXUBEE, BUTTA-HATCHIE, WOLKEE part of MOBILE make;

TANGAPAHOE, PEARL and TIPSAW, STRONG and
AMITE meet in Lake.—
Somber waters, somber borders, where the languid
saurian dwells
'Neath the live oak's mossy mantle and the grand magnolia dells.

NOTES ON THE RIVERS OF MISSISSIPPI.

	See Note		See Note
Sunflower	109	Pasca-Gouli	118
Talla-Hatchie	110	Tulla-Homa	114
Yazoo	111	Bough-Homa	114
Yalla-Boosha	112	Esca-Tappa	107
Loosa-Scoona	89	Ocktibbehaw	116
"Flitting 'Father'"	113	Noxubee	119
Homa-Chitto	114	Butta-Hatchie	105
Pierre	115	Wolkee	120
Tippa	116	Mobile	108
Hatchie	110	Tangapahoe	121
Buckatoona	117	Lake	122

109. SUNFLOWER. The Sunflower River is simply an overflow of the Mississippi, a debouchure from the main current. The Indian name of the stream was SOCK-TAFFA-TOOTA. "Taffa" is doubtless the same original word now written both "Tappa" and "Tippa," and just as Jaffa and Jappa are the same. The name Java appears to be an etymological equivalent. See Note 116 for the term "Tappa."

110. HATCHIE. The term "Hatchie" has been heretofore referred to as the old Seminole and Muscogee word for river. It is found in the British possessions and also in South America in prehistoric nomenclature, but invariably in connection with some other term either a synonym or a modern descriptive. It is used in the appellative sense alone only in this instance and in the name of the same river in Tennessee. "Talla" is supposed to mean the muddy. See Note 73.

111. YAZOO. There is in Russia a river with the same original name, the word rendered from the Russian symbols either Yazwa or Yazoo. The true word is Ya-soo, or Ya-su, a composite with the two synonyms—Hebrew "Ya," and the Oriental term "Su," river—seen in our river name Sioux in its French garb. Another Russian name reproduced in Mississippi is Wolkee.

112. YALI-BOOSHA. "Ya-li" is the same as "Wa-li," water flowing. The most remote form of the term is in the Hebrew of the Edenic name Au-wau-li, this in the Anglicism Havillah.

The Edenic word is found in its absolute purity in the old Shoshone dialect of the Pacific Coast, where it is given as the tribal term for river. The word survives in the appellation of the two rivers coming together in Eastern Oregon, "Walla-Walla." "Wa-li" is the old Anglo-Saxon original of our word "well" as applied to a fountain of waters. As "Ya-li," the term is in the Chinese, the word we now have as "Yellow," the Chinese name for a sea and a river. The Alabama river name now known as "Yellow Water" I am satisfied was originally Ya-li Wattee, a native Indian name. The term "Boosha" is supposed to be a mere dialectic expression. A corruption of the initial term is seen as Yu-lee in a number of Indian names on the continent.

113. "Flitting 'Father.'" The Mississippi is sometimes called the "Father of Waters," under the supposition that its name signifies this fact. The tradition doubtless comes from one of the old titles given by De Soto, the discoverer, as CHUCK-AUGUA. This name shows some analogy to the Choctaw term for the Deity, CHIHOWA, and the Delaware Indian equivalent, JE-HO, or CHE-HO. There is an interesting tradition connected with this word, which may not be inappropriate here. This legend states that far back in the ages the finger of the Great Spirit touched the primeval mountain wall at the place now called the "Delaware Water Gap," cleaving a passage eastward for the waters long imprisoned beyond. Henceforth the river was known to the aborigines as "GOD'S RIVER," the idea expressed in the Delaware tongue in the ancient aboriginal title of the river CHI-HO-OCCI, the term for river in the suffix "Occi," this evidently a corruption of *Ogha* or *Aqua*. For further reference to the name Mississippi, see Note 130. Chuckauga is the true word now written Chicago.

114. HOMA-CHITTA. The term "Homa" has been referred to in paragraph 4, the "River Name," and also in Note 95. Chitta is supposed to be a corruption of the word "Chatta," meaning owl. See Note 76.

115. PIERRE. The pronunciation is Pe-ayr. It is supposed to be a native name, the term "Aar" found in many of the native appellations. See the "River Name," paragraph 8. The term "Pe" is in the South Carolina name Pee-Dee.

116. TIPPA. Etymologically, this word, as Tepa, denotes sim-

ply deep water. It is doubtless the same original term which is seen in the native names of our waters in the diverse writings Tippee, Tibbee, Tybee, Tappa, and Taffa. This is the only instance in which it is found alone in the appellative sense; in all other cases it is in a composite with other terms; these in most instances mere synonyms, as in the name Tippa-canou and its near identity Kantappahaw. The oldest form of the word known is in the Hebrew name of a water originally written En-Tappua, the term "En" referred to in paragraph 13, the "River Name." The Syrian name is now written Tappuah. We see the same original word in the name of a city of France, by the deep waters of the sea, the word written in the French idiom Deippe. The term "Tippa" is also in the old Irish nomenclature, in the name Tipperary.

117. BUCKA-TOONA. The term "Toona" in this name shows analogy to the German word for Danube, Doonaa. It is the ancient name Dena in corruption. See Note 12.

118. PASCA-GOULA. The term "Goula" here is doubtless but a corruption of the word Gauli, referred to Note 18. "Pasca" is the same as the term written "Pasquo" in the name of the North Carolina river Pasquo-tank.

119. NOXUBEE. The term "Ubee" is evidently the same as the California name Yuba. The term is seen also in the Hebrew word for river, Yu-ba-li. Note 29.

120. WOLKEE. This name is identical with the Russian appelation written either Volga, Wolgee, or Wolka. We see the same word in the Georgia appellation Okee-wolkee.

121. TANGAPAHOE. The term "Tang" is referred to Note 5. The suffix "Apahaw" is found in the Georgia name Alapahaw. Apa-haw is simply river.

122. The rivers named all go to Lake Ponchartrain, in Louisiana.

THE RIVERS OF LOUISIANA.

From the Pearl to Sabine westward, by plantation and savanna,
And her rice-lands, gulfward lag the sluggish streams of Louisiana.
Here's Chifuncte; and here Bogue-chitto; Sara, too, with cypress stain;
Tangapahoe, Amite, Comite, Tickfaw;—all to Pontchartrain.
Here are Grand, Lafourche, the lazy; Terra-Bonne with spreading bayou,
Teche and Crocodile here crawling on to red Atcha-Falaya.
Creeping through the diked cane-lands goes Vermillion to the Bay;
Farther westward, still and lonely, Mermenteau and Calcasieu.
From the far northwestern border comes, through yielding ochery bed,
Rio-Roxo, with her driftwood wonder, fitly named the Red;
Saline, Black-Lake, Cane, and Bodceau by these currents filled and fed.
Southward, washing through the loamy, fertile vales of Arkansas,
With Bartholomew and Tensaw and the Boeuf, is Ouachita.

THE RIVERS OF LOUISIANA.

Here the mighty Mississippi, half a hundred fathoms deep,
In his plash a hundred rivers still their fretful murmurs keep;
"Gathered" here the countless waters, half of all a continent,
Seething, like a serpent writhing, all in awful volume blent.
From the Black Hills and the lake-lands, and from eastern oil and coal lands;
From the Appalachian summits, and from western grain and gold lands;
From the cañons of the Rockies, 'neath the never-going snow;
From rich prairie, and from desert where but sage and cacti grow;
Past a hundred crowded cities, through the forest's silent hush;
Fled from fearful height and boulder, and the frothing cascade's rush;
By the cot and painted palace, from the wigwam of the savage;
Through the peaceful Southern bayou, from the western floods and ravage;
Gathered in one vexing volume, artery of a continent;
Seething, like a serpent writhing, all in rolling grandeur blent.

NOTES ON THE RIVERS OF LOUISIANA.

	See Note		See Note
Bogue-Chitto	123	Calcassieu	127
Sara	124	Red	126
Tangapahoe	121	Arkansas	128
Comite	125	Ouchitah	129
Teche	125	Mississippi	130
Atcha-Falaya	126		

123. BOGUE-CHITTO. Bogue is a word found in prehistoric nomenclature in different countries. See Note 4, also Note 76 for Chitto, supposed to be a corruption of Chatta.

124. SARA is a term for river, a sibilant form of Aa-ri, found in use in the appellative sense in many ancient tongues. Its oldest form is in the Hebrew, where it appears as the name of a noted water, the fountain near which Abner was slain by Joab. The title survives yet in the Oriental name *Ain Sara*. The name Syria owes origin to the same root-words. The ancient term is seen in the prehistoric names of a number of waters in America, nearly all of whom have their exact prototypes in the names of the Old World. Our lake name Saratoga, with its term "Taqua" as "Toga," and indicative of the deep waters, is the counterpart of the Russian appellation written either Sara-toga or Sara-towka. Our name Sara-nacca, with its Hebrew Nachar as "Nacca," is the same as the ancient name of the Ægean Sea, Saronika. See Note 49 for "nakar."

125. AMITE, COMITE, and TECHE. These are doubtless survivals of the French influence in the nomenclature of Louisiana, this long a French province. There is a river named Tesh (Tech) in France.

126. ATCHA-FALAYA. This in pronunciation is Atch-a-fal-ly-ya, rhyming with *by-yu* (bayou). Atcha-falaya is the old Indian name of the Red River. Authorities say that it denotes in the native tongue the "Lost River." This tradition is confirmed by both physical and verbal facts. We have already seen in numerous citations that the term "Atcha" was used by the aborigines in the sense of river. The suffix "Falaya" shows

striking analogy to a form of the ancient word seen in the Latin *falor*, which means to lie hidden or concealed from view. This is precisely a condition which formerly existed in this river, a condition referred to in the expression " Driftwood wonder," well known to geologists and others. Up to quite a recent date the current of the stream for nearly a hundred miles of its course was hidden from view by vast and deep masses of driftwood and soil, which, for unknown centuries, had been accumulating above the waters. Growing out of this mass of drift were large forests of trees several feet in diameter, when the country first came into the possession of the United States. Years of time and toil, and millions of public money have been expended by our government in efforts to remove the obstructions and open the river to successful navigation. It was in this part of the river that a disaster befell the national troops under Gen. Banks in 1863. The old Spanish and French name of the river was Rio-Roxo: this, Anglicized, gives the modern appellation the "Red River." The current is fitly named: the waters are of a rich ochery red, the fact due to the immense quantities of clay and red soil held in solution, the coloring coming from the " yielding ochery bed."

127. CALCASSIEU. This is a French version of the native word, the modern pronunciation Cal-cash-ya, or Cal-cas-sha, the accent on the last syllable. The term "Cal," found in many of our native names, is referred to in Note 147. Cassia, or Cashee, is found as the native name of waters in North Carolina and Idaho.

128. ARKANSAS. The true word is Aar-Kansaw. See Note 30 for the term "Aar." The suffix " Kansas" survives in the name of another river. The writing in a final silent "s" is due to the old French influence.

129. OUACHITA. This is the old French writing of the native name we now have as Washitaw and Wichita, the word rhyming with Arkansaw. The varying orthographies illustrate the principle in language heretofore referred to, showing the identity of French *Oua*, or *Eau*, and the English or German *wa*. Ouachita is simply the river Chatta, the word " Chatta " said to mean "owl" in the native tongue. Etymologically the term " Chatta " is really Cha-te, the initial showing the Oriental term cha, tcha, tsa, denoting water. It is also a remote

form of our word sea. We see this Oriental term in its composite with the root-word for the deep, "De," as the ancient lake name written Tchade or Tchad. Another form of the word is in the original name of a deep water in Louisiana, Caddo. A kindred expression is the Spanish name written Cadiz. The full name as OUACHITA, in its queer French garb, has its exact prototype in the Russian name seen on our maps as Ouichitza.

130. MISSISSIPPI. This is another of our American names over which there has been much speculation. The modern writing of the word is known to have been the fanciful coinage of a French priest in the seventeenth century. The journals of De Soto, the first white man to discover and give authentic versions of the native appellations of the water, records various tribal designations of the stream. It was known, says that authority, in 1540, as RI, as CHUCK-AUGA, as MICO or MESSO, as MES-APA, and otherwise. The French explorer Allouez, in 1665, gives the writing MESS-IPPE. This is substantially the same as one of the names given by De Soto more than a century previously. Marquette, in 1673, gives the form of the word as METCHE-SEPE. The term "Sepe" is a known synonym of "Ippe." There is tradition that the true word meant "The gathering together of the Waters." Certainly the physical facts are in confirmation of the legend, given, I think, in Barnes' School History of the United States. The waters of a large portion of North America are finally borne to the gulf through the mighty stream. The term for water in the name is well understood—this is in the expressions, "Pa" or "Apa," "Ippe" or "Sepe." The feature of the word indicative of the "Gathering," the descriptive or adjective in the name, must therefore be looked for in the initial of the different writings, "Mess," "Messo," or "Metche." Geological facts come to our aid in determining the problems connected with the words. The true river is regarded as being in the current known in the upper part of its course as the Missouri. This was written originally, when the name was first made clear, Mes-ouri. The suffix "Ri" in this name is also well known as a native term for river, a near synonym with the suffix in the name as Messis-apa or Messa-pi.* These facts show that the

---

* And also one of the true names of the river.

two names Mississippi and Missouri are substantially the same thing in significance. The term "Mes" as it occurs in our English is traced to the root of the Latin words *Meto* and *Messis*, and whence come our words meter and measure, denoting, in the original sense, a gathering together. The participle of the term Meto, Messui, denotes the "gathering." The name Messui-Ri would therefore denote "the gathering river;" an expression tersely characterizing the stream, since it gathers into its mighty embrace the waters of so many different lands. The term "Ri," as De Soto has told us, was one of the appellations, while his writings "Mico" (Messi) and "Messapa" give us a suggestion as to the true descriptive in the composite appellation. A remote type of the name given by the discoverer is seen in the Oriental word Meso-potamia.

THE RIVERS OF TEXAS.

To the dark gulf, never resting, tossing whitecaps o'er its green,
Coursing 'twixt the RIO GRANDE and the RED and brown SABINE,
Drag the dreamy Texas rivers: NECHES first, with ANGELINE;
Then the Indian's AAR-KO-KEE-SA, TRINITY, through forest flows;
Next their OU-REE, SAN JACINTO, where the star of Houston rose.
Through the rolling mesquite prairie, where the wild dog builds his town,
BRAZOS, once the TOCK-ON-HONA, winds and waits and wanders down,
Bearing with him NAVASOTA, BOSQUE from the bottoms brown,
And PALOXY, GABRIEL, NOLAND, and KEETUMSEE.
—Farther west
The slow SAN BARNARD seeks the deep and troubled briny breast.
Then from Llano Estacado, through the barren mountain shadow,
Over sandstone, granite, marble, to perennial blooming meadow,

Flows the ancient PASHO-HONO, now the Spaniard's
COLORADO;
In its current mixing CONCHO, LLANO, stony PERDI-
NALLES,
And SAN SABA, from the sand plains, and PECAN
from nutty valleys.
Next with NAVADAD, LAVACCA; then the purple
GUADELOUPE,
Where there rang in war times deadly, savage Santa
Anna's whoop,
Where blend BLANCO and SAN MARCOS through its
mossy stone-bed run,
And the COMAL, glittering brightly as the dewdrops
in the sun.
In the ancient city springing, SAN ANTONIO darts
away,
With SAN PEDROS and CIBOLA and MEDINA to the
Bay.
MISSION and AARANSAS, FRIO with SABINAL, HONDO
deep,
LEONA, NEUCES, and SAN MIGUAL, ATASCOSA, wind
and creep
Where the cacti spread in splendor, and coyotes revel
keep.
To DEL NORTE purls the PECOS; and from where the
savage paints,
Scalping cowboys, small SAN PEDROS, he and various
other "SAINTS."

Eastward trails the gloomy CYPRESS; snail-like SULPHUR's in the pines;
And ATTOYAK mid cottonwood, eastward, noiseless lags and winds;
Eastward HEE-CHEE-AQUE-HONO, PEASE and WICHITAS are whirled;
And the long and red CANADIAN, like a pennon, is unfurled
In the northlands from the red man's war-camps in the sunset world.

NOTES ON THE RIVERS OF TEXAS.

	See Note		See Note
Neches	131	Guadeloupe	140
Trinity	132	Comal	141
San Jacinto	133	Aaransas	132
Tock-on-hona	134	Hondo	57
Navasota	135	Neuces	36
Llano-Estacado	136	Del Norte	142
Colorado	137	Pecos	143
Concho	138	"Saints"	144
Perdinalles	139	Hee-chee-aque-hono	145
Navadad	135	Wichitas	146

131. NECHES. The local pronounciation is Na-ches, the accent on the "Na." This is doubtless the same aboriginal word given elsewhere as Natches. There was an ancient tribe of Indians called by the name Natches, and said to have been white, or of the Caucasian color. They were doubtless the last remnant of an aboriginal stock—the Tuscaloosa chieftain the last representative of a black race. See Note 100. The modern Indian is apparently a mongrel, or a cross between the white European and the black Moor. Columbus states in his journals that he discovered Moorish traits among the natives at the time of his first landing. The usually beardless face and the long, straight and coarse black hair of the American red man have their types in the Moor. Ethnologists, as a rule, do not regard the Indian as a pure Mongolian.

132. AAR-KO-KEE-SEE. The TRINITY was originally known by this name. The word is found also as OR-QUIS-ACO. See Note 30 for the term "Or" or "Aar." The expression "Quisacco" is found in the South American "Chu-quis-acca," the native name of the La Platte.

133. SAN JACINTO. It was on the banks of this river, in 1836, that Gen. Sam Houston, commanding the Texas armies of the Revolution, won his first great victory over the Mexicans; this established the independence of the Texas Republic. It was indeed here that the "Star" of the illustrious hero arose. The native name of the river was Ou-ri or Ouree, a name that survives in the appellation of a river in Colorado,

the word now written Ouray. See Note 30 for the term "Uree."

134. TOCK-ON-HONA. This is given as the native name of the Brazos; while the original title of the Colorado was PASHO-HONO or PASHAW-HONAH. The term "Honah," seen in the different Texas appellations, appears to be but the aspirated form of the word "Au-na," referred to in Note 7, the writing in the superfluous H representing the Spanish idiom. The word Brazos is Spanish, denoting the brown; while Colorado, in the same tongue, is the red. The names have been interchanged in the historic era: the title Colorado once applied to the river now known as the Brazos; the latter name belonged to the Colorado. The changes occurred while Texas was a Mexican province. The term "TOCK" is an abbreviation of Toccoa or Taqua. See Note 61.

135. NAVASOTA. The term "Nava" is doubtless the same ancestral word seen in the writings of the Indian names in Napa, Naba, and Nawa; and seen also in the Old World river name Nava—this written either Nava, Neva, or Nieva. "Sota" appears to be simply a sibilant form of the word "Au-de" or "Ota," referred to Note 45. This term is found in the Indian names both as a final and as the initial—as in the appellations Sota-yoma (the native name of the Russian river of California) and in Minne-sota.

136. LLANO ESTACADO. The Spanish expression denoting the Staked Plains.

137. The COLORADO is one of the most interesting of all the rivers of Texas. It presents in its course a wide range of scenery. Entering Southern and Central Texas, it is the first river that can be heard running at any considerable distance during all seasons of the year. The current is subject to sudden and dangerous rises from unknown subterranean causes. It has been known to increase several feet in height in a few minutes, and without any note of warning in the way of rainfall. The subterranean outflow is pure and clear. The old Indian name of the water was Pash-aw-Hona. The term "Pashaw" has its exact type in the river names of the old world, the most remote form of the word being in the Hebrew Pashawna; this the Edenic appellation rendered "Pison" in the Anglicism of the Biblical record.

138. CONCHO. This is doubtless the same word we have in the South Carolina name Conga-ree—the Texas name in the Spanish idiom. See Note 47.

139. PERDINALLES. The term rendered "Nalles" is doubtless the word Nau-li, in the foreign idiom—the final S superfluous. See Note 154. The term "Perdi" is evidently the same as that in the initial of the Florida name Perdi-do.

140. GUADELOUPE. The Texas name is doubtless but a reproduction of the old Spanish appellation, referred to in paragraph 12, the "River Name." The composite factors in the word, however, are seen frequently in the Indian nomenclature. For the Moorish term "Guade," see Note 48; for "Oupa," see Note 78. On the banks of the Guadeloupe the Mexican general, Santa Anna, massacred a large body of Texan troops surrendered as prisoners of war. Hence the reference "savage Santa Anna's whoop."

141. COMAL. The Comal is one of the brightest of all the American waters ever seen by me (and I have seen more than half of the rivers of the United States. I have crossed every stream named in Texas, with but about half a dozen exceptions. More than three-fourths of the other Southern rivers have been seen and studied, and the local pronunciation of the names learned by me in the immediate vicinity of the waters themselves. These statements are made not in the spirit of egotism, but that they may aid in emphasizing the authority of the work).

142. DEL-NORTE. The full title of the river is RIO-GRANDE-DEL-NORTE, of the old Spanish writing. This, in English, is the Grand River of the North.

143. PECOS. This pronunciation is Pa-cos, accent on "Pa."

144. There are in Western Texas several small streams having, in the old Spanish titles, the term "San" or "Saint," all the streams flowing to the Rio Grande.

145. HEE-CHEE-AQUE-HONO. This long Indian name is said to mean "River of the Prairie-Dog Towns." In the old Mexican tongue the river was called also Palo-Duro.

146. WICHITAS. There are two rivers known as Wichitah. Wichitah and Washitaw are the same—the old French Ouachita. See Note 129.

THE RIVERS OF TENNESSEE.

Tennessee! How were her rivers in the olden Indian tongue?
What syllabic rhythm had they ere the white man's changes rung?
Wasciota and Shewanee, thus the Cumberland was known;
With Red, Caney, Obee, Harpeth, and the Sulphur, New, and Stone.
Holston once was Hogee-hee-gee; and, from mouth of French Broad down,
Which was once the Taqua-Osta, Cootcla on to Chota Town,
This an Indian "Refuge City" of an ancient, wide renown,
Where there emptied in Tenassa, this the Little Tennessee;
Then began great Kalla-Muckee, Chalaqua in Cherokee.
Once Hiawassie was Euphassie, with its brawling, small Chestoa,
Esta-Nauli, "Where they rested," and Amoah or Occoee.
Through Chilhowee comes the Little, this the Red Man's swift Canou;

Where the wingless PIGEON flutters, once the AGAQUA they knew.
Where Unaka sent his daughter, SALACOI, is TELLICO;
Where was once the NAULI-CHUCKEE simply CHUCKY now we know.
Thundering through the Alleghanies with the DOE is yet WATAUGA;
Out and in, with Georgia pranking, straight to Gulf goes CONNESAUGA;
Out, but never more returning, "Stream of Death" is CHICKAMAUGA.
Down through Alabama rattling, ROCK and FLINT and ELK they go,
White man's rivers, they and SANDY, DUCK, BEECH, BUFFALO.
But SEQUATCHIE keeps her beauty from the "vandal changes" free;
OBED and the dancing DADDEE, these glide on to EMOREE.
Where is now the CLINCH with POWELL, once was known as PELLOS-IPPE;
CHUCKAUGA, REE, MES-APA, all these were names for MISSISSIPPI;
Thither going NANNA-CONNA, LOUSA-HATCHIE, FORKED-DEER,
WOLF, OBION with his REEL-FOOT, and BIG HATCHIE hieing there.

By these waters fought the Shawnee, Uchee, Choctaw, Cherokee,
Chickasaw, and Chickamauga, Tuscarora, Muscogee.—

Dead are all those tawny warriors; but the music of the river
And the sweet syllabic rhythm of its name shall live forever!

FROM PHOTO.
SAN FRANCISCO. CAL.
DEC. 1885.

CAPT. M. V. MOORE,
NATIVE TENNESSEEAN,

NOTES ON THE RIVER NAMES OF TENNESSEE.

	See Note		See Note
"White man's changes".	147	Doe	161
Shewanee	148	Watauga	162
Obee	149	"With Georgia pranking"	163
Taqua-Osta	150	Chickamauga	164
Chota Town	151	Flint	165
Tenassa	152	Sequatchie	166
Hiawassie	153	Obed	149
Esta-Nauli	154	Pellos-Ippe	167
Occoee	155	Chuckauga	168
Canou	156	Lousa-Hatchie	170
Pigeon	157	Wolf	172
Salacoi	158	Obion	149
Tellico	159	Big Hatchie	169
Nauli-Chuckee	160	Muscogee	171

147. Effort is made in these verses to rescue from oblivion, and, if possible, properly preserve in this work the old native appellations of some of the rivers of Tennessee now having modern titles. The aboriginal names still in existence are, in many instances, known corruptions, fanciful versions, or merely conjectural forms of the native words. Those who have heard the red men of America in the utterance of their words understand well how vague and unsatisfactory are their enunciations, and especially in the vowel sounds. It is also difficult to distinguish the difference in G and K, in D and T, and P and B, on the native tongue. And hence it is that we have among the old words such a wide variety of English writings of the remote originals, these also in many instances conjectural expressions at best. A single vowel ending in a native appellation has been given different writings with the English letters A, Ie, Ee. Our sound of U has been rendered in " Indian " names Ou, Oo, U, Ieu, and Eau. The name Tennessee in the now adopted orthography is known to be a fanciful coinage from an original word written both Ten-assa and Ten-essa. We pronounce the word with a strong vocalization and accent on the last syllable. And yet the old native pronunciation of the word, as Ten-is-a, with accent on the first syllable, is still

remembered by many who heard the name as it had come directly from the native tongue, the vocalization of the other syllables so indistinct as to admit of the varied writings. The true appellation has been also misapplied. The name Ten-assa— Tennessee, as we now write it—did not belong originally to the chief river of the state as it now does. It was the title of the stream now known as the Little Tennessee. The old Cherokees, who were the most numerous and influential of all the tribes occupying the territory at the time the English colonists first came to the country, called the main river CHALAQUA. This title applied from the mouth of the Ten-assa down to the Ohio. A dialectic title among some of the natives was Kallamuckee. The two appellations are substantially the same: Chal-aqua appears to be the pure remote word, the aboriginal coinage; while Kalla-muckee is a tribal or dialectic expression, a corruption of the original. The term "Muckee" denoted in the native mind the idea of "Big Water," or "Much Water;" while the form of the expression as "Uckee" or "Aqua" was simply water or river. Forms of the same terms appear in the writings "Muchee" and "Uchee," the name Kallamuckee surviving yet in the Georgia creek appellation now written Callamuchee. The term as "Muckee" survives in the native appellation of Nevada, Winne-Muckee, a deep lake there. (The term "Winne" is referred to in Note 55.) The ancient word CHALAQUA has been perverted in modern writings. It is the true original of the name we now have as "Cherokee." In old chronicles the word is written *Chel-akee* and Kelakee. The old Cherokee Indians did not use the letter R in their dialect. They were called "Cherokees" by the neighboring tribes, who used the sound of R as the equivalent of L, as do the Japanese of to-day. The term "Chal," or "Kal," as it appears in the dialectic expression, is supposed to have referred originally to that part of the Tennessee River now known as the "Mussel Shoals," and where the current seethes and boils so about the vast limestone ledges in its bed that it has localities named in the common parlance of the boatmen on the river, in such homely and significant expressions as the "Pot," the "Frying Pan," the "Skillet," the "Sucks," etc. The term "Kal" is supposed to have been inserted in the original composite word as a descriptive of these features of the river as they appeared on the native mind. The word is an ancient expression, the remote root whence come our English words coal, caloric, etc. In its original significance the root-word appears to have denoted heat, energy, vehemence, etc. It is in a number of the native appellations of American waters that are noted for their warmth—as the Calousa, of California; as the Caloosa, of Florida—or for their boisterous energy, as the Tennessee. In Ramsey's "Annals of Tennessee," the author, quoting from Adair, says that the name Cherokee is derived from a word (Cheera) signifying fire. This is analogous with caloric, heat.

148. WASCIOTA and SHEWANEE. These were the native names of the Cumberland, known in different dialects. Wa-Sciota was simply the River Sciota, the suffix now seen in the appellation of a river in Ohio. The Cumberland was also known as the Wari-ota, the two ancient synonyms "Wari" and "Ota" in the one word. (See paragraph 8, the "River Name.") The name as Sewanee is preserved in the title of the great university on the summit of the Cumberland Mountain. The modern appellation of the river is in honor of the English Duke of Cumberland. The old French writing of the name Shewannee was *Shavaunon*.

149. OBEE. The word is written usually Obey. It is supposed to be a corruption of the ancient term "Au-ba," or "Obi," as it appears in the Russian. Three Tennessee names show the old Oriental term: Obee, Obed, Obion. The latter is doubtless Obi-anna. See Notes 29 and 7.

150. TAQUA-OSTA. This was the native name of the French Broad. See Note 23. Ramsey gives the name of the French Broad as *Agiqua;* others give this as the name of the *Pigeon*, a tributary of the French Broad. See Note 157.

151. Chota Town. This was an ancient city of refuge used by the aborigines. It was situated at the mouth of the Little Tennessee where there was an easy crossing on a shallow shoal of the main river. There is now no vestige of the ancient city surviving, but the name "Chota" still remains in the appellation of the "Shoal" so well known to boatmen on the river. Elsewhere on the continent the aborigines had their cities of "refuge" governed by the same laws as those which obtained among the Jewish nations of antiquity. See Note 62. How and by whom the ancient Hebraic institution was introduced

into America will never be known. We have seen, however, that the two peoples—the ancient Hebrews and the old colonists of the New World who named its waters—held in common many words, both full names and terms, words that appear to have possessed similar significance in the respective tongues. From Chota Town up to the mouth of the French Broad the native name of the river was COOTCLA. This appears to have been simply a mere dialectic expression, its significance unknown. Above the French Broad the river now known as Holston was called in the Indian tongue HOGEE-HE-GEE. The term "Hogee" is doubtless simply an aspirate form of the corruption "Okee," river; "Heegee" is an unknown dialectic word.

152. TENASSA. This name has been referred to Note 147. The word is supposed to mean the "Long River," the stream having for its size an unusually long and winding course through the mountains of East Tennessee and Western North Carolina. The term for river is in the writing "Assa," the purest known form of the primitive word now seen in the old Anglo-Saxon term written usa, ousa, etc. (Note 73.) The Greek term for the sea, Thal-assa, referred to in Note 103, and the Hebrew word Massa reveal the expression. Another form of the word is seen in Note 153.

153. HIA-WASSIE. The original name of this river appears to have been simply Assie, or Wassie. To this appellative different tribes added their dialectic terms for river, giving us four different composites which history and tradition have preserved as the ancient names of the river. These are HIA-WASSIE, EUPH-ASSA, NA-QUASSA, and RE-QUASSIE. The names give evidence of the synonymous character of the different initials "Hia" (seen in both Hebrew and Chinese); "Euph," seen in the Greek (of Euphrates) and the Russian (of Oufa) and the germ-words "Ri" and "Na." In Note 155 we find other curious evolutions in the prehistoric tongue.

154. ESTA-NAULA. Tradition says this word signifies the place or water "where they [the Indians] rested." The term "Nauli" is seen in two of the Tennessee River names, this and the old appellation Nolly-Chucky, now simply Chucky. The word is found in the Hebrew, in the term for river written in the English letters either Na-hali or Na-auli. We see in this word the remote form of the name Nile, through its Latin garb

Nilus. The name Esta-nauli has a corruption in the writing Oustenaulee, referred to in Note 65. The initial term in the name, "Esta," appears to refer to rivers or countries where the natives "rested," or where they spent the summer months in hunting and fishing, and away from the low altitudes and warmer latitudes, where they had the winter homes. It is a curious fact that this same term "Esta" is found also in the Latin where it has reference to the summer months. A pure form of the word is in the Alabama creek name Esta-boga, and in the North Carolina name Esta-Toah (see Note 22); while corruptions are seen in the names Oustenauli, of Georgia, and Taqua-osta, of North Carolina. In old chronicles the word is written Oostinahli. Nah-li is a correct form of the Hebrew written Nahal, or Nahauli.

155. OCCOEE. This river was called by the old aborigines also AMOAH. The latter name appears to be a corruption of an original word for water or river seen in the Hebrew in the writings Ya-ma, Amaa, and otherwise similarly. A corruption of the true word is seen in the Oriental river name given on our English maps in the writings Amou, Amoo, etc. Another very singular and striking fact in connection with this name is that which shows that the Oriental river known as the Amou was known also to the ancients as Occoa or Accha, the modern writing of the name in the Greek idiom being Oxus, the Hebrew as Accho. The final vowel sound in A denotes the peculiar idiom of the Indian. In some of the old maps of the country, the name of the river is given as Aquoke, a word which appears to be simply a different dialectic expression of the same original word whence comes Occoe and Occoa. Aquokee applied to the Toccoa also.

156. CANOU. This was the native name of the river now called the Little. The word Can-ou meant originally in the Indian tongue the Caney River. See Note 15. It is found in the composite name of a river in Indiana, Tippa-Canoe. The word "canoe" as applied to a "dug out" boat, is simply a borrowed term, applied without reference to the original meaning, as many of our best English words are. Authorities give the word as an "Indian" term for river, but in the grotesque writing *Key-nough.*

157. AGAQUA. This was the native name of the river now

called the Pigeon. The significance appears to have been "river where the fields are," places in the valley of the river long cultivated in corn by the Indians. The stream was known also as the Wah-na or Wau-na. See Note 7 for wauna.

158. SALAQUOI. The name is spelled variously in the suffix. The true writing is doubtless Sal-aqua. The word appears to be congeneric with Saluda. See Note 45. This was the leaping river, the stream springing out of the high places in Unaka Mountains. This name Unaka, unquestionably a native Indian word, is singularly like the Latin *Unica*, and our English unique.

159. TELLICO. See Note 53.

160. NAULI-CHUCKY. This is the full writing of the name now given in the abbreviation simply Chucky. "Chucky" is said to have been a dialectic word in the Cherokee tongue meaning "dangerous." The term "Nauli" has been referred to in Note 154. The ordinary writing is "Nolly."

161. DOE. There are two theories in regard to this name. One confounds it with the name TOE or TOAH, the North Carolina river name referred to Note 22, the two streams having their sources near together. Tradition states that the name "Doe" was applied to the river by the great hunter, Daniel Boone, in commemoration of the fact that he had killed an unusually large female deer on the banks on the river. It is known that he once had a hunting-camp at the head waters of the stream, and under the shadow of the Roan Mountain. This famous peak of the Alleghanies, its very highest point, received its title from a noted old roan horse belonging to the hunter. The animal strayed away from the camp one fall, but was found next spring, fat and sleek, on the summit of the mountain on the rich, grassy "Bald."—I have these facts from an old pioneer of East Tennessee, Christian Razor, who died about 1852, aged over ninety. He had known Boone personally. This man Razor claimed to have been the first man who ever brought a wagon across the Alleghanies from North Carolina into Tennessee.

162. WATAUGA. See Note 61 for the term Taugua. A similar name is in Alabama, the writing Autauga. The words appear to have no significance except that of river.

163. "With Georgia pranking." The Connesaugua runs in

and out across the Georgia state line several times before finally making for the gulf through the Coosa of Alabama. All the other rivers of the state go to the gulf through the Mississippi, the majority of their currents first emptying into the Ohio. The oldest writing of the name now known as "Connesaugua" is found in the journals of De Soto, where the word is written *Canasaqua*. See Note 15 for the term "Can."

164. CHICKAMAUGA. This word is said to mean "River of Death." There are, however, no reliable *data* sustaining the tradition except that the native Indians known as the "Chickamauga tribe" were the most cruel and bloodthirsty of all the savages who once roamed over this section of the country. The "tradition" is evidently the coinage of a modern fancy, taking advantage of the terrible issues of blood and death occurring on the banks of this river in September, 1863. The initial term in the name is found in many of the native appellations of America—as Chicka, Chico, and Checo. As Chico, it is a California name. "Mauga" is doubtless the same original word that now appears in the corruptions "Mucky," "Mohawk," etc., referred to Note 147. Doubtless the purest form of the word known is in the writing *Mah-aqua*, which the historian George Bancroft gives as the aboriginal title of the Hudson, the word surviving in the corruption Mohawk. The significance of the expression *Mah-aqua* was simply "Great River."

165. FLINT. The native name of this river was CHEE-WALI, the word written also CHU-WAULA. The Alabama creek name Chee-wa-clee is a kindred expression. The term "Wau-li" has been referred to in Note 112. The term "Che," seen in many of the ancient appellations of America, has its prototype in the river nomenclature of the Old World. In the English writings Tche, Tchai, Tsai, Tsa, there is a Turkish word for river, the word supposed to have been evolved from the sibilant form of the Hebrew Yaa as Sa. In the more modern tongues of the Old World the term is seen in the writings Sa, Su, Sjo, Zee. Our own English word "sea" has the same remote origin whence comes all the forms of the words here given. The modern Turkish word for river written simply Su, is reproduced exactly in the native name of one of the American rivers written in the French idiom Sioux.

166. "Vandal Changes." The historian Ramsey, in "Annals of Tennessee," says that the supplanting of the old native appellations by the modern title was an act of "vandalism." The name Sequatchie has various writings, and a number of "traditional meanings." Its final term "tche" is referred to in Note 165. The word Sequoa is given as a native California word now referring to big trees, and also to a noted chieftain.

167. PELLOS-IPPE. This was the native name of the Clinch River. The title "Clinch" owes its origin to the exclamation of an early explorer who, falling into the waters of the stream, and unable to swim, cried to a companion to "clinch" him, and prevent his drowning. Pellos-ippe is the dark water. The term "ippe" has been referred to in Note 130. It is a native term for water or river. *Pellos* shows identity with the Greek and Latin word *pellos*, denoting dark-colored. The waters of the Clinch are supposed to owe their dark tinge to the stains coming from the many coal-bearing strata about the sources of the river.

168. CHUCK-AUGA. This word is given by De Soto, the discoverer, as one of the native names of the Mississippi. See Note 130. The name Chicago is a modernized form of the word. The significance of the expression was not, in the native language, "Windy City."

169. HATCHIE. Our authorities on the native languagues of America give the word Hatchie as a term for river in the Seminole and Muscogee dialects. While the word appears to have been used by most of the Southern Indians, it is found also in the British America name, Sax-atcha-wan, and in the New York appellation, Oswego-atchie. The term is found usually in connection with another factor. This is the only instance in which it appears alone as the appellative. "Hatchie" is evidently but an aspirate form of the same word which is seen in the Celtic as *Acha*, in the Italian as *Aci* (atchie), and in the French as *Aix*. In the old dialects of the British Islands the same word is written *Axe*, *Exe*, and *Uxe*, a term for water or river, but used as an appellative. Axe and Exe are river names in England. As Ouche the name is in France; as Ouchy in Switzerland; and as Oochee in China. We have the word in our Indian nomenclature as Uchee, Ucha, Uchi. The names Jujuy, a river of South America; Ujjiji, a lake of Central

Africa; and Ujjijai, a town of Spain, are apparently simply variations of the same ancestral word.

170. LOUSA-HATCHIE. The term Hatchie is referred to above; " Lousa " in Notes 89 and 100. The latter is found in different parts of the world in the prehistoric river nomenclature. In the English transcripts from the Russian and Central African names, the writing is Louza. We find the term in the Indian names both as initial and also as the final, as in Lousascoona, Tusca-loosa. The word owes origin to the germ *Lu*, the flowing, and *ousa*, water. See Note 103 for *Thalassa*.

171. MUSCOGEE. The native accent was originally on the last syllable; but in the modern tongue we hear it also as Mus-co-ga, with the accent on the second syllable. The word was originally written Mus-qua-kee.

172. WOLF. Ramsey, in " Annals of Tennessee," gives the native name of this river as " Margot." A final syllable has evidently been suppressed. The true word doubtless was *Mahgotah* or *Magota*, the etymological equivalent of the South-American name, Bogota.

THE RIVER NAME:

ITS ORIGIN AND HISTORY.

As the majority of the aboriginal river names of America are supposed to have been coined from types preexistent, and now seen in the Old World languages, it is apparent that the primitive colonists of the New World, who named its waters originally, had either a knowledge of those types or a knowledge of the verbal science and art revealed in the structure of the words. It will be well, therefore, to glance briefly at the known history of the Old World words, before we can appreciate fully or properly the character of the native Indian names of America.

1. The history of the Water and River Nomenclatures of the Old World is sufficiently well known to etymologists to have enabled them to determine and specify distinctly the verbal roots or germ-words in human language out of which definite terms and names were coined by the primitive man for the expression of ideas and facts in connection with the subject. It is supposed that many of the primordial root-words now seen in our language had their origin mainly in the principles of onomatopy—in the suggestive expressions of the things or phenomona to be named. Objects in rapid motion—and especially machinery, certain birds, as well as currents of water—make a peculiar sound, which is quite fitly expressed in our word "whirr"—with two Rs. It has been observed that in most English words indicative of the idea of rapidity of motion there is the letter R—as in rush, run, whirl, race, etc.

Kindred expressions are seen in writings with the kindred letter L—as in fleet, flitting, flow, etc. The majority of ancient terms for river, or stream of flowing water, contain a root-word having one or the other of the letters R or L. Etymologists have given these root-words, in their primordial forms, the English writings " Ri," " Ru," " Rha," or similarly otherwise with the letter R; the germ in L being " Li," " Lu," or " Flu." The Greek form of the word denoting primarily motion is in the writing " Flu," out of which has grown a large family of words having reference primarily to movement. In combination with an ancient germ-word for water, written in English both " Wa " and " Va," the term "flu" makes the word for river seen in the pure English idiom as *flu-wa* or *flu-va*, or in the Greek and Latin idioms *fluvios* and *fluvius*. Forms parallel with these words, and showing the germ-word in R, give the term for river as *ri-va* or *ri-wa—rivus* of the Roman idiom. In the Spanish idiom the same word is *ri-oo*—the expression " Oo " the exact synonym of " Wa " and " Va," the latter representing the Teutonic idioms, while the writing as " Oo " comes from the ancient Basque form of the word for water, this now denoted usually in the French idiom as Eau, sometimes Eu.

2. The very oldest of all the written forms of the ancient germ-words for water are found in the Hebrew. The generic word for water in that language is written in our letter M—the full expression either Mo, Maa, Aam or Yaam. The origin of the Hebrew term for water in the symbol English M is traced to a word written variously in the ancient Hebrew as Yaam, Yom, Yaama, Aa-Ma and Ho-Ma, this being the expression

which the Mosaic record gives as the name applied by God, the Creator, in the morning of time, when He gathered the waters together, and called them seas. Out of the initial sound in this divine word for the "gathered waters," there appears to have been evolved all those syllabic expressions denoting primarily water, and seen now in the Hebrew writings in the English forms as "Yeo," "Ya," "Y," "U," "Ai," "Hai," "Owa," "Oah," and reproduced in the modern English writings from the ancient languages and dialects of Western Europe and the British Islands also as "Yeo," "Eo," "Ae," "Eau," "Ou," "Aa," "Ah," "Wa," "Va," and otherwise. Authorities give about twenty different writings of the one word as a term for water in the ancient European languages. As "Aa," "Au," "Aue," "Yeo," "Eu," "Wye," "Vie," and "Y," it has survived as the name of more than thirty European rivers and other streams—the appellations being prehistoric.

3. In the ancient Oriental languages the symbol for water is given in characters which correspond to English P and B. In the Sanskrit the full writing of the word for water is either Ap or Pa, or more fully as Ap-aa, a form seen in the old Wallachian or Dacian tongue, which is supposed to have perpetuated the pure word in its entirety. In the Arabic and Persian the word for water is in the writing with the labial B, as Ba, or Au-Ba. In the ancient Egyptian tongues the writing was in M as in the Hebrew—this labial the symbol generally for most of the Semitic tongues. The full writing in the Coptic was Mu or Moo, this form seen in the old Turkish. In the pure Hebraic the writing was either Maa or Mo.

4. The primordial germ-word indicative of the idea of depth, as relating to waters, appears in the ancient languages of the Old World in the English writings both as "Te" and as "De." The oldest form of the word deep is in the Hebrew, where it appears as Te-Am, or Te-ho-ma—the aspirate H in the Hebrew without true etymological value. The real and full significance of the word, in Hebrew, is *deep waters*—the term "Am" or "Homa" denoting, in that tongue, waters. The idea of perpetuity, as this relates to the motion of waters in the river or other stream, was denoted in the ancient Old World tongues, in our English writing, "Na." The fact is illustrated in the Hebrew name Ama-na, the exact equivalent of the Arabic form of the word as Aba-na—the river known in the history of Naaman. The word is given a translation in Isaiah, where it is rendered as waters which are perpetual. (Chapter lviii., verse 11.)

5. These facts show us that the ancient river nomenclature of the Old World contained only six or seven primordial germ-words. Out of this brief store the primitive nations of mankind wrought their words, both terms and names, for water and river. In what age of the world these germ-words became generally known is a problem indeterminate. It is a fact, however, that each and all the primordial words I have named are contained and illustrated in the river names of Eden—words which were doubtless coined by Adam himself.

6. In order to enable the reader to revert to the facts in future references, and in a prompt and convenient view, the following epitome of the above paragraphs, is made, showing at a glance the germ or root words,

with their significance as used in ancient river nomenclature:

Mo, or Maa, Ba, or Aub, Ap, or Pa, are the labial forms of the primitive word for water.

Au, Eeu, or Yeo, Ya, or Hai, and Wa, and Va, are vowel forms of the word for water.

Te or De denotes the idea of the deep in connection with water.

Ri, or Li, and their idiomatic forms "Ru," "Wra," "Rha," "Flu," and "Flo," indicate the fact of motion as connected with waters.

Na denotes the idea of perpetuity of motion in waters.

7. In some of the ancient languages the labials were all used interchangeably. The fact is especially true of the Hebrew, in which tongue the labial germ-word for water appears as frequently in B and P as in M, in all composite expressions. As the individual symbol for water, the letter M alone was used.

8. In the list of expressions representing the vowel germ for water, there is doubtless but one true original—the others being mere idiomatic forms of the ancestral word—this supposed to have been the Hebrew AU. There are four different ancient writings of the term, these supposed to have been coeval in origin—the variations doubtless due to national idiom or to the mere conjectures of copyists, or translators, in supplying vowels in words originally written only in the consonantal symbols. In a composite with the germ word "Ri," the running, the word appears in the old Egyptian Coptic and Hebrew terms for river, now seen in the English versions as Yu-bali, Yeo-ri, Au-ri, and Eia-ro. The last three are all the same word unques-

THE RIVER NAME. 101

tionably, but in varying idioms. The modern Turkish idiom shows the term as Ya-ro—a form seen also in the native Australian river name Yara-Yara. Another form of the same term is in the Celtic word for river written either Aar, Ayre, Ahre, or Ayr. This is regarded as the true original of the river names of Western Europe and the British Islands now written Ayr, Ohre, Aure, and Ayre. The old Chaldee corruption as Ur or U-re is found in prehistoric names of rivers in nearly every part of the world. It is conspicuous in the river nomenclature of the aborigines of America, two rivers of the United States having this old Chaldee word as the native title: the Ouray of Colorado and Ouri of Texas. The term is seen also as the suffix in the name Missouri. All forms of the term appear in the names of Southern rivers, as we see elsewhere in this work.

9. The history of river nomenclature shows that originally in the primitive tongue of the nations the water received no other title than that which conveyed the idea simply of water, or water in one of its varying conditions of depth or motion. Streams were named before the purely descriptive adjective or the mere honorary term was known in connection with waters. But we now find ancient appellations which are composites showing two or more actual synonyms in their structures. Indeed, in some of the oldest names for waters in existence there is this feature of the word: it contains pure synonyms. Even the river names of Eden are no exception to the rule.

10. The majority of the names of antiquity showing the two synonyms in the one word originated in this way: Originally—as I have just said—the water bore

a title that was simply a national term for water or stream, the word representing the idiom of a tongue corrupted (or "confused," in the Scripture expression). It was doubtless an effort to reproduce a remote original perverted in the Divine purpose at Babel, as well as resulting from the imperfections of human memory, which alone, for countless centuries, kept the words until the art of writing was finally invented. In a subsequent age, and on the occupation of the various countries by new peoples speaking a different language from that of the primitive colonists, the old names were not supplanted; but they were referred to in the terms for water or river in the tongue of the new nations. In process of time the two terms—the old and the new—grew into the one appellation. Examples are known where there are as many as three synonyms in a single name of a water. The words afford curious and valuable studies not only in language, but also in human history otherwise. The very footsteps of the ancient migrating man, of extinct tongues and extinct nations, have been traced over continents by the shreds of language left in the nomenclature of the countries.

11. The history of the river names of Spain affords some of the most interesting and valuable illustrations of the facts just referred to. Take, for instance, the name we have on the maps of that country as Guadelquiver. The original title of that water was Chebar or Kabar. This was a Hebrew term for river, used in the days of Ezekiel, in the appellative sense, as the name of the stream upon which the prophet began his career. In some unknown age of the world the word was borne to the west of Europe, and applied as the name of the water in Spain. In the conquest of that coun-

try by the Moors of Africa they applied to the old preexistent title their national term for "the river"—this being "Wady," *river*, and "el," *the*—the full expression becoming "Wady-el-Kabar." In the Spanish idiom—which writes the English sound of "Wa" in the letters *Gua*, and gives "Ka" as *qui*, and V for B—the Moorish phrase of three words is converted into the single beautiful appellation Guadelquiver. This one word reveals the touch of three distinct and different tongues—the modern Spanish, the Arabic Moor, and the remote unknown Semitic—this latter representing a race of people who, hundreds of years before the advents of the Romans and Christianity, colonized Western Europe, and left in the languages there the scores of Hebraisms and other Oriental terms now found in the ancient river and water nomenclatures of the country.

12. The Arabic or Moorish influences in connection with Oriental forms of speech are to-day visible in much of the river nomenclature of Spain. The interesting appellation Guadeloupe is the Arabic "Wady-el" (the river) with a suffix in a corruption with the Sanskrit Ap-aa (water) as "Oupe." This corruption has two well-known forms—the old Slavonic as "Ou-pa," or "U-pa," and the Greek as "Eu-pha," or "Eu-fa," seen in the name Euphrates. This latter is one of the river names of Eden, not in its Hebraic form, but retained— as many of the Biblical names have appeared—in the English versions of the Scriptures, in their old Greek and Latin idioms, and not at all times in the pure Hebraisms. The true Hebrew of the word, as Greek Euphrates, originally written only in the symbols corresponding to English P-R-T, appears fully in the

writing as Aa-pa-ri-te—this a form of the word corresponding with its oldest expression in the Greek of Herodotus—before the days of the Hellenic classicism. The corruptions "Ou-pa" and "Oo-fa" are found in many of the prehistoric names of waters, and especially in Russia and the Southern states. We have had occasion to revert to this fact in a number of the Notes of this work.

13. There is also another Oriental term for river seen frequently in the names of the waters of Southwestern Europe, to which we have had occasion to refer in numerous Notes. This is the word found in the Persian as "Ain," and in the Hebrew as "Ain," "On," "Au-na," and frequently as "En" simply—as in the names En-rogel, En-Gady, etc. The suffix in this latter Hebrew brook name is identical with the Arabic term "Wady" above noticed. A curious fact, and one well illustrating the history of river names, is that which shows that the name Ain-Gady, with its composite factors in inverted order, is the same as the Spanish river name now written Guadi-anna. The pure and full form of the latter term was in the Hebrew in the pronunciation as "Au-na," the abbreviation as "En" and "On" simply an Anglicism. We have seen this Oriental term, "Au-na," in a number of its Old World forms in the native Indian names of waters in many instances. And even the Arabic term, both as "Watte" and "Guati," is conspicuous in the appellations of the aborigines of the continent—some of the facts given in the Notes. "Au-na" is the germ-words Au, water, and Na, the perpetually flowing.

14. One more Oriental term seen in the native names of America deserves a reference before we dismiss

the subject. It is seen with a composite factor in the Russian name Dneiper. This word is an English abbreviation of the true word in the Slavonic as Dena-apri, or in the French idiom as Danapris. This name has the two synonyms, "Dena" and "Apri." "Dena" is the word which we see so frequently in the river names of the Old World in the writings "Don," "Dan," "Tan," "Ton," "Doon," "Dun," and otherwise similarly. Its oldest form is in the Hebrew river name written in the Scriptures Dan, and in the modern Arabic Dahn, the word applying originally and yet to the deep fountain which in the Syrian hills is the wonderful source of the river known as the "Dan." The name occurs in the Biblical annals in a period five hundred years anterior to the birth of the man Dan. Its companion "Ap-ri" in the Russian appellation is an Oriental term for river showing origin in the germ-words Sanskrit "Ap" and "Ri"—these also the ancestors of the kindred Latin term "Ri-pa," synonymous with "Ri-va," river. A very interesting and striking fact in connection with the name Dneiper is that which shows that it is substantially the identical word which appears in the Greek idiom as Borysthenes. This is the old Arabic title of the river, rendered in the English equivalents of the Greek letters. The original name of the river was simply "Dena." In other words, it was once one of the "Dons" of Russia. The national term "Apri," applied as the suffix to the primitive appellation by the Orientals, giving the name Dena-apri, or Dneiper. The Southern Arabs, whose national term for river has been for many centuries "Ba-ri," or simply water running—the word frequently written "Bahr," "Bar," and "Bor," applying their word as the prefix, the full expression became Bari-Dena. This in the Greek idiom is, as I have just said, Borysthenes. The true Arabic name is discovered still in the English writing of the name of a great city on the banks of the river, Borodina, made memorable by the terrific battle fought there by Napoleon in the disastrous Russian campaign. The term " De-na " is simply a composite of the germ-words De, the deep, and Na, the perpetually flowing. The word as " Dee " was used in the appellative sense by the ancient colonists of the British Islands as the name for rivers. An old Scottish corruption is in the writing " Tay." The term " Tau," found also as the river name in England, and also as the native Indian name of a river in North Carolina, appearing furthermore in numerous composite appellations of rivers in the Southern states, is not regarded as precisely the same word. It shows origin in the two germs or root-words " Te " and "Au." A further reference to this expression is made in Note 20. The aborigines of America appear to have used the word " Dee " in the same sense in which it is found in the old Anglo-Saxon or Scotch name, expressive of the deep water or deep river, but usually as a suffix, as in the names Sand-Dee (Santee, Note 50), Pee-Dee, etc.

15. The limits and purpose of this work forbid a fuller discussion of the history of river nomenclature in these pages. What has been written is given solely with a view to making clear in the mind of the reader some of the problems which appear in the Note references to the river names of the aborigines of America, and especially in connection with some of the Indian appellations of the Southern states. Nowhere on earth are the ancient Old World terms for river and water

seen with a greater degree of distinctness and accuracy than in many of the names that have been long regarded as the coinage of the " savages " of America. I do not pretend to advance any theory in these pages as to the primitive sources of the words; there is no wisdom of to-day that can show clearly whence came the knowledge of the ancient pioneers of the Western World who first named its waters. I simply place on record in my pages the facts as gleaned from historic archives. In regard to the conclusions which may be drawn from the premises, the reader is entitled to his or her own opinions. I shall not make the work a vehicle for the expression of my individual views here.

www.ingramcontent.com/pod-product-compliance
Lightning Source LLC
Chambersburg PA
CBHW030407170426
43202CB00010B/1521